United States
Department of
Agriculture

Forest Service

Pacific Northwest
Research Station

General Technical
Report
PNW-GTR-816
May 2010

Effects of Fire, Insect, and Pathogen Damage on Wood Quality of Dead and Dying Western Conifers

Eini C. Lowell, Valerie A. Rapp, Richard W. Haynes, and Caitlin Cray

Authors

Eini C. Lowell is a research forest products technologist, U.S. Department of Agriculture, Forest Service, Pacific Northwest Research Station, Forestry Sciences Laboratory, P.O. Box 3890, Portland, OR 97208-3890. **Valerie A. Rapp** is a science writer, P.O. Box 383, Blue River, OR 97413. **Richard W. Haynes** is a retired economist, Forestry Sciences Laboratory, Portland, OR. **Caitlin Cray** is a former forester, Bingen, WA.

Cover photographs: see figure 18 on page 71 for photographers' credits.

Abstract

Lowell, Eini C.; Rapp, Valerie A.; Haynes, Richard W.; Cray, Caitlin. 2010.
Effects of fire, insect, and pathogen damage on wood quality of dead and dying
western conifers. Gen. Tech. Rep. PNW-GTR-816. Portland, OR: U.S. Department of Agriculture, Forest Service, Pacific Northwest Research Station. 73 p.

We update and expand the 1992 survey of research findings by Lowell and
colleagues, providing an ecological context for the findings, using a more reader-
friendly format, and including extensive citations so readers can get indepth
information on particular topics. Our intent is that managers will use this report
as a desktop reference and field guide. The worksheet can be copied and taken to
the field, as a reminder of key indicators to look for and key questions to ask. With
a visual assessment process, potential volume and value losses associated with
disturbance can be estimated for postdisturbance management planning.

Keywords: Fire-killed stands, fire-damaged stands, insect damage, pathogen
damage, wood quality, wood deterioration.

Contents

Introduction

Droughts, wildfires, and insect and disease outbreaks have left large numbers of standing dead and dying trees in western forests. Forest inventories conducted by the U.S. Department of Agriculture Forest Service estimate the average annual mortality volume (i.e., the volume of wood in the trees that die or are killed each year by natural causes) to be about 2,500 million cubic feet (USDA FS 2005, 2006). Management of these dead and dying trees, in particular postfire salvage, is controversial (Peterson et al. 2009). The idea of managing dead and dying trees is an integral part of forest management, arising from the dependence of modern society on wood products such as lumber and paper, and societal concerns about the ecological well-being and perpetuation of western forests. Ecological, economic, and cultural—some would add spiritual—values are involved. Forest managers strive to balance all these values in their decisions, but often there are significant differences in how residents, stakeholders, and local communities perceive risks and appropriate responses. Regardless of point of view, most people agree that accurate scientific information is critical for sorting out the multiple, sometimes conflicting, values and making good decisions.

Many factors influence deterioration rates of fire- and beetle-killed conifers.

Key among these decisions are those in developing management regimes for landscapes with significant dead timber. These require information about what effect fire, insect, and pathogen damage have on wood quality of dead and dying conifers. Many factors influence the deterioration rates of fire- and beetle-killed conifers, and thus influence the volume and quality of wood available from these conifers. We summarize research on how fire, insects, and pathogens affect the wood quality of common conifer species in the Western United States (Alaska, Arizona, California, Colorado, Idaho, Montana, New Mexico, Oregon, Utah, Washington, and Wyoming) and western Canadian provinces. We also summarize what is known about the rate of deterioration for these tree species, the factors influencing the rate, species-specific changes in wood quality, and potential suitability of the wood for commercial use. Our focus is on the first 3 to 5 years after a wildfire or beetle attack causes tree mortality. This information may be useful as one factor among many affecting postdisturbance management decisions.

We update and expand the previous survey of research findings in Lowell and colleagues (1992), providing an ecological context for the findings, using a more reader-friendly format, and including extensive citations so readers can get indepth information on particular topics. Our intent is that managers will use this report as a desktop reference and field guide. Appendix 2 lists references by species for those that need detailed information, such as equations for determining volume and value loss. The worksheet and accompanying reference photo guide (app. 3) is provided as an insert to this report so it can be taken to the field, as a reminder of key indicators to look for and key questions to ask.

This report is divided into five sections. In the first section, we briefly review the changing context for managing dead and dying conifers. These changes are altering information needs. The following section provides a review of previous studies. In the third section, we synthesize information about how fire contributes to forest mortality. We then summarize wood quality changes, by species. Finally, we synthesize the relations between wood quality changes and economic values.

The Changing Management Context

Changing societal objectives for public land management and episodic levels of dead and dying timber have combined to raise interest in the ecological role of dead and dying conifers in western forests. Managers find themselves struggling with how to balance the typical wood utilization timeframes of 3 to 5 years with ecological timeframes that often extend for decades. Contributing to the struggle has been a lack of information that describes the ecological role of dead and dying timber that can be used in postdisturbance planning. Here we briefly summarize some of the information that addresses a number of issues important for postdisturbance planning. These include legacy contributions of dead and dying timber; the effects of fire on understory plants, soil properties, wildlife species, and air quality; and management concerns. Later we focus on how these factors relate to changes in wood quality of dead and dying conifers. Our purpose is to provide information to managers as they consider their opportunities to develop management plans for dead and dying timber.

The legacy contributions of dead and dying timber have become important considerations in various ecosystem management approaches. Managers are encouraged to consider the organic matter and nutrients in dead and dying conifers and how they contribute to postdisturbance recovery of forests. Complete decomposition of fallen trees can take anywhere from decades to centuries, depending on location, and research so far has been mostly on the first few years of that process. One tool that has been developed to help managers is DecAid Advisor.[1] It is a Web-based tool for managing snags, partially dead trees, and down wood for biodiversity, including postfire conditions in Oregon and Washington. These findings are relevant both for understanding the ecological roles of dead conifers and for understanding wood quality changes in dead conifers when wood recovery

---

[1] DecAid Advisor can be found online at http://www.fs.fed.us/r6/nr/wildlife/decaid/index.shtml. The Web site's multiple layers allow users to quickly find succinct summaries, and then locate underlying references and data, if desired (Marcot et al. 2004, Mellen et al. 2009).

is being considered. Although it was prepared specifically for Oregon and Washington forests, much of the information is relevant for other areas.

The effects of fire on understory plants and fuel loads were discussed by Brown and Smith (2000). Their purpose was to assist managers with ecosystem and fire management planning. They described postfire plant community developments in North American ecosystems and ecological principles of fire regimes. Brown and Smith (2000) also discussed the implications for postfire management in an ecosystem context and emerging issues related to climate change.

Fire affects soil, water quality, and waterflows. The effects on soil properties and hydrological cycles, in particular, can be long lasting. Neary and colleagues (2005) reviewed these effects, including the physical, chemical, and biological effects of fire on soil properties, soil biology, water resources, water quality, hydrological cycles, and watershed rehabilitation. Reeves and colleagues (2006) examined the ecological issues related to postfire harvest in riparian areas. They pointed out that postfire salvage may not help to restore riparian structure and function, and that fish and other aquatic and riparian life often recover in just a few years after a fire. However, the potential effects of any salvage in riparian zones depend strongly on the landscape context and disturbance history of the area.

Wildlife are of great concern after a large wildfire. Smith (2000) discussed which wildlife species flourish after large wildfires, benefiting from the loss of forest cover, increase in forage, increase in snags, and other habitat changes, and which wildlife species decline, affected by the loss of live trees and understory shrubs. Saab and colleagues (2007) discussed the effects of prescribed fire on bird habitat and populations of the interior West; much of this information would also apply to wildfire effects.

Looking at wildlife without backbones (invertebrates), Black (2005) discussed the ecological roles of insects that feed on conifer needles or tunnel into conifers, including bark beetles, Douglas-fir tussock moths, and western spruce budworm (see app. 1 for common and scientific names). He discussed how these various insects change forest structure, influencing tree density and tree species diversity, and also influencing disturbance regimes. In addition, his report examines the effectiveness of different ways of managing insect outbreaks.

Smoke, soot, and ash are the obvious effects of fire on air quality. Much research has been done to quantify the smoke and emissions produced by prescribed fires and wildfires, the effects on public health and ecosystems, and the transport and dispersal of smoke and emissions. Sandberg and colleagues (2002) reviewed all these effects of fire on air quality, including the science behind air quality regulations and the transport of fire emissions.

Note that Brown and Smith (2000), Neary and colleagues (2005), Sandberg and colleagues (2002), and Smith (2000) make up a four-volume set of general technical reports from Rocky Mountain Research Station. The set is a good foundation for a reference library on wildland-fire effects in western ecosystems.

Mazza (2007) summarized the main management concerns after a large fire, which "include minimizing erosion and its effects on aquatic systems, retaining adequate forest structure for fire-associated wildlife, capturing the economic value of the wood through postfire timber harvests, minimizing the likelihood of an insect outbreak among fire-stressed trees, reducing the potential for a severe reburn, and ensuring tree regeneration."

Postdisturbance management options need to address the concerns and attitudes of local communities.

Key concerns have been the effects of postfire salvage logging on fuel loads and reburn potential. The sheer number of variables—forest type before wildfire, burn severity, fire regime, and postharvest slash treatment, to name just a few— means that no one answer will fit all cases (Mazza 2007). Peterson and colleagues (2009) provided a good synthesis of current science on the effects of postfire timber harvest after large wildfires in western North America.[2] Mazza (2007) offered a short, easily readable summary of the Peterson and colleagues (2009) synthesis. Thompson and colleagues (2007) found that in a southwest Oregon mixed-conifer forest, salvage logging and planting after the 1987 Silver Fire did not reduce the risk of high-severity fire when the 2002 Biscuit Fire reburned the area 15 years later.

Complicating the management of postfire and other types of disturbances is the need to understand and address the concerns and attitudes of local citizens. There is growing evidence that the residents, stakeholders, and local communities have multiple perceptions of both risks and appropriate responses and that these seldom mirror those of land managers (Flint et al. 2008). This suggests a need to first understand the concerns of local citizens, as well as the issues of regional or national organizations, and further, to include concerned people effectively in planning. Olsen and Shindler (2007) reviewed the growing literature on agency-citizen interactions after large wildfires. They discussed five major themes from the research: contextual considerations, barriers and obstacles, uncertainty and perceptions of risk, communication and outreach, and bringing communities together. Their publication suggested ways for managers to involve people in planning and restoration after a large wildfire. In the case of postfire timber

---

[2] Peterson and colleagues (2007) provided an excellent reference on the many vegetation and fuel management tools now available. Some of these tools are useful in postfire management planning as well. The Peterson and colleagues report gives detailed summaries of the tools, including data requirements, specific uses, and level of user knowledge required. It also gives examples of how the tools can be integrated into actual planning and used at different steps and for different needs.

harvest, Lindenmayer and Noss (2006) pointed out that it takes place in different conditions from harvest in unburned forests and therefore may have different effects. Their article discusses these possible effects, including loss of biological legacies, changes in plant communities, and effects on landscape patterns, among others. They suggested developing well-informed policies before large fires occur, so policies can be carried out in a timely way when fires do occur. Flint and colleagues (2008) found in the case of mountain pine beetle (MPB)-killed timber in Colorado that as local groups begin to perceive the impacts of "red and dead"[3] trees on forest goods and services (timber, recreation, scenic views, etc.) they value, they begin to form responses to the risks as they understand them (fig. 1). These responses also include dealing with specific hazards to infrastructure such as standing dead trees next to houses, roads, and power lines. Second, these responses will differ among communities. High-amenity communities may be

---

[3] The ongoing MPB outbreak has introduced the description "red and dead" to describe forests under attack. The red trees are thought worth salvaging for products whereas the dead trees might be cull and would preclude their being financially feasible to harvest.

Figure 1—Beetle infested (red) and beetle-killed trees at the wildland-urban interface.

more concerned with aesthetic and attendant economic changes. Communities with a resource extraction orientation may be more concerned with forest operations responses to changing forest conditions (and the ability of local managers to organize such responses). This work has shown a growing tolerance for timber harvesting of dead trees and some green trees for firebreaks in proximity to communities and homes. In more remote areas, the higher the amenity rating, the lower the tolerance for large-scale timber harvesting.

Previous Studies on Effects of Disturbance on Wood Quality

Interactions among fire, insects, and pathogens in conifer forests play a critical role in wood utilization opportunities postdisturbance. Parker and colleagues (2006) has an excellent discussion of this, with a focus on the interior Western United States and western Canada. The publication also discusses the ecological roles of forest insects and pathogens, including diversifying forest structure, thinning forest stands, creating wildlife habitat, cycling nutrients, and so forth. Finally, it examines how high fuel loads and dense forests can change these interactions, and how the widespread use of prescribed fire to reduce fuels might change these interactions in the future.

Many variables influence the effects of postfire salvage logging. Quoting again from Mazza (2007), "The timing of timber harvests after fire (same season as fire vs. subsequent years, winter vs. other seasons) can affect the magnitude of ecological and economic effects. Mortality to regenerating trees and understory vegetation is lessened if timber harvests are conducted shortly after the fire. Harvests within this timeframe also produce the highest wood volume and quality for commercial uses."

The older studies on rates of wood deterioration have considerable variation in methodology. The methods used are not always clear in older publications. The term "volume" is not clarified, so it is unclear if authors are describing total cubic volume, bole volume, sapwood volume, volume after bark slabs removed, or other possibilities. Also, site conditions are not always specified, leaving uncertainty about site influence on the findings. Finally, the older studies do not always specify how defect was measured or what measurement (scaling) system was used. Today's market offers new possibilities for wood products such as engineered wood composites and small-dimension products, but the older studies report almost exclusively on dimension lumber products.

Older literature often deals with stands that would now be classified as old growth and with large-diameter trees (Beal et al. 1935, Boyce 1929, Kimmey 1955).

These studies often refer to "young trees" for small-diameter trees, and "older trees" for large-diameter trees. However, trees grown under active management may achieve the diameter of the so-called "older trees," but have a higher proportion of sapwood than trees of equivalent size in the older studies. Because the proportion of sapwood is an important factor in the rates of decay and deterioration, the findings from older studies may not always apply precisely to contemporary stands. Not all information from older studies on large-diameter trees is included here, because the salvage of such trees is often not part of contemporary practices.

Another feature of previous studies is that they typically only addressed volume loss in fire-killed trees. Lowell and Cahill (1996) measured volume loss in trees for 3 years following wildfires in southern Oregon and northern California for Douglas-fir, true fir, ponderosa pine, and sugar pine. Among recent studies, Hadfield and Magelssen (2006) studied 750 fire-killed trees of seven species for over 5 years and documented changes owing to char, insect attack, fungal growth, and weather. Tree species studied were Douglas-fir, Engelmann spruce, grand fir, lodgepole pine, ponderosa pine, subalpine fir, and western larch. Each year, up to 150 of the study trees were cut for detailed measurement of decay. The study design resulted in good, detailed data. However, all study trees were on five wildfire sites in eastern Washington, and different conditions on other sites may cause different rates of deterioration. Jackson and Bulaon (2005) documented changes in fire-killed larch from one area in northwestern Montana. For all these studies, no products were manufactured to assess utilization volume and value loss.

Overall, Hadfield and Magelssen (2006) found that changes in fire-killed trees differed greatly by tree species. Their report gives findings on percentage of volume affected, but not on suitability for various wood products. The report summarizes: "Ponderosa pine and lodgepole pine had most of their sapwood stained one year after death. Thick-bark tree species, ponderosa pine, Douglas-fir, and grand fir were attacked rapidly by wood boring insects and decayed more quickly than thin bark species. Thin bark species cracked very quickly but were slower to break than thick bark species because they decayed slowly." Detailed findings from Hadfield and Magelssen are included throughout this document.

Other studies focus on specific issues and address wood product recovery. For example, Aho and Cahill (1984) examined the deterioration rates of windthrown conifers in the maritime climate of western Oregon and Washington. One of their objectives was to "help resource managers plan salvage operations on Mount St. Helens." Fortunately, salvage after volcanic eruptions is not likely to be a common situation, but the Aho and Cahill study is a useful reference for managing windthrown trees. Several species of beetle-killed trees have been studied. Lowell and Willits (1998) looked at lumber recovery of dead lutz (a white and Sitka spruce hybrid) spruce from the Kenai Peninsula, Alaska, and Lowell (2001) reported on veneer recovery from this same resource. Parry and colleagues (1996) sampled Douglas-fir and grand fir that had been killed by beetles, not by fire; also, their study was specific to the Blue Mountains of eastern Oregon. Effects of white pine blister rust mortality on wood utilization were reported (Snellgrove and Cahill 1980) as were effects of mountain pine beetle mortality on lodgepole pine (Fahey et al. 1986). Lewis and Hartley (2005) prepared a synthesis on deterioration of wood quality and quantity as part of a larger project addressing mountain pine beetle mortality. Product-recovery studies on fire-killed trees are few and have focused on ponderosa pine (Fahey et al. 1990, Lowell and Parry 2007).

Beetles can cause mortality in surviving trees.

Douglas-fir beetles and wood borers influence the rate of decomposition of Douglas-fir logs (Edmonds and Eglitis 1989). A study by Edmunds and Eglitis was done on the western slope of the Cascade Range in Washington, with pairs of newly felled, unburned Douglas-fir logs, using screening to keep insects away from one log in each pair. They found that the rate of decomposition slowed in logs that insects were unable to access. Wood borers had more influence on log decomposition than Douglas-fir beetles.

The effects of ambrosia beetles, bark beetles, and wood borers have been studied in Douglas-fir, western hemlock, Pacific silver fir, and western redcedar logs on the western slope of the Cascade Range in Oregon (Zhong and Schowalter 1989). Ambrosia beetles channeled into Douglas-firs and western hemlocks, and only during the first year after tree death. Bark beetles tunneled in the Douglas-fir phloem (layer just inside the bark) and Pacific silver fir phloem, also during the first year only. Wood borers attacked only Pacific silver firs during the first year, and then all tree species in the study except Douglas-fir during the second year. The ambrosia beetles and bark beetles inoculated the dead trees with different assemblages of decay fungi, which produce different decay patterns and may influence long-term patterns of decay.

After the Fire: Changes in Dead and Dying Conifers

One of the first questions asked after a fire is which trees will die over the next several years from their fire injuries, and which trees will survive. A closely related question is how many trees, and which trees, are likely to be killed by bark beetle attacks in the first few years after the fire. The prediction of how many trees will die after the fire is fundamental for postfire decisions on hazard tree felling, salvage logging, reforestation, and wildlife habitat (Brown et al. 2003). Some tools exist to help managers predict the mortality of fire-damaged conifers.

Predicting Conifer Mortality Following Fires

Tree survival is influenced by some of the same factors that affect tree deterioration. Thick-barked trees can survive more scorch than thin-barked trees. Wagener (1961) found that merchantable, young, fast-growing trees on good sites have the best chance of surviving a fire.

Indicators used to predict the survival of fire-damaged trees include fire intensity, extent of crown scorch or crown consumption, extent of cambial damage, bark char height, extent of needle consumption, season in which fire occurs, and bole diameter of the tree (Bevins 1980, Dieterich 1979). The amount of rainfall during the next growing season and the presence or absence of bark beetles are also factors (Bevins 1980, Dieterich 1979). Ryan and Reinhardt (1988) and Ryan and Amman (1994) also used bark thickness in predicting mortality for seven western tree species (fig. 2a).

Sieg and colleagues (2006) produced a model to predict the 3-year postfire mortality of ponderosa pines, based on data from over 5,000 trees in four burned areas in Arizona, Colorado, Montana, and South Dakota. The study found that the percentage of crown scorch and the percentage of crown volume consumed, considered as independent variables, were the best predictors of mortality (fig. 2b). An example from the paper shows why the two variables must be gauged separately. A ponderosa pine with 20 percent crown consumption plus 20 percent crown scorch has a greater than 40 percent probability of dying in 3 years. However, the authors explain, "if that 40 percent crown damage was 40 percent scorch and no consumption, the probability of dying is less than 30 percent." If the damage was 40 percent consumption with no scorch, the model predicts the tree has a more than 65 percent chance of dying within 3 years.

The robust results for the Sieg and colleagues (2006) pine mortality model suggest that their two-variable model based on percentage crown scorch volume and crown consumed volume will likely be useful beyond the intermountain West.

Recent research has found some of these indicators to be better predictors than others. Hood and colleagues (2007) produced a guide that describes models and variables significantly influencing Douglas-fir mortality after fires or bark beetle attack (fig. 2c) and includes a cambium kill rating variable (number of tree quadrants with dead cambium at ground level). A photo guide shows examples of fire-damaged trees and describes how to measure injury severity in the field. See also Hood and Bentz (2007), for models predicting the probability of Douglas-fir mortality and Douglas-fir bark beetle attack, based on fire injury and stand characteristics.

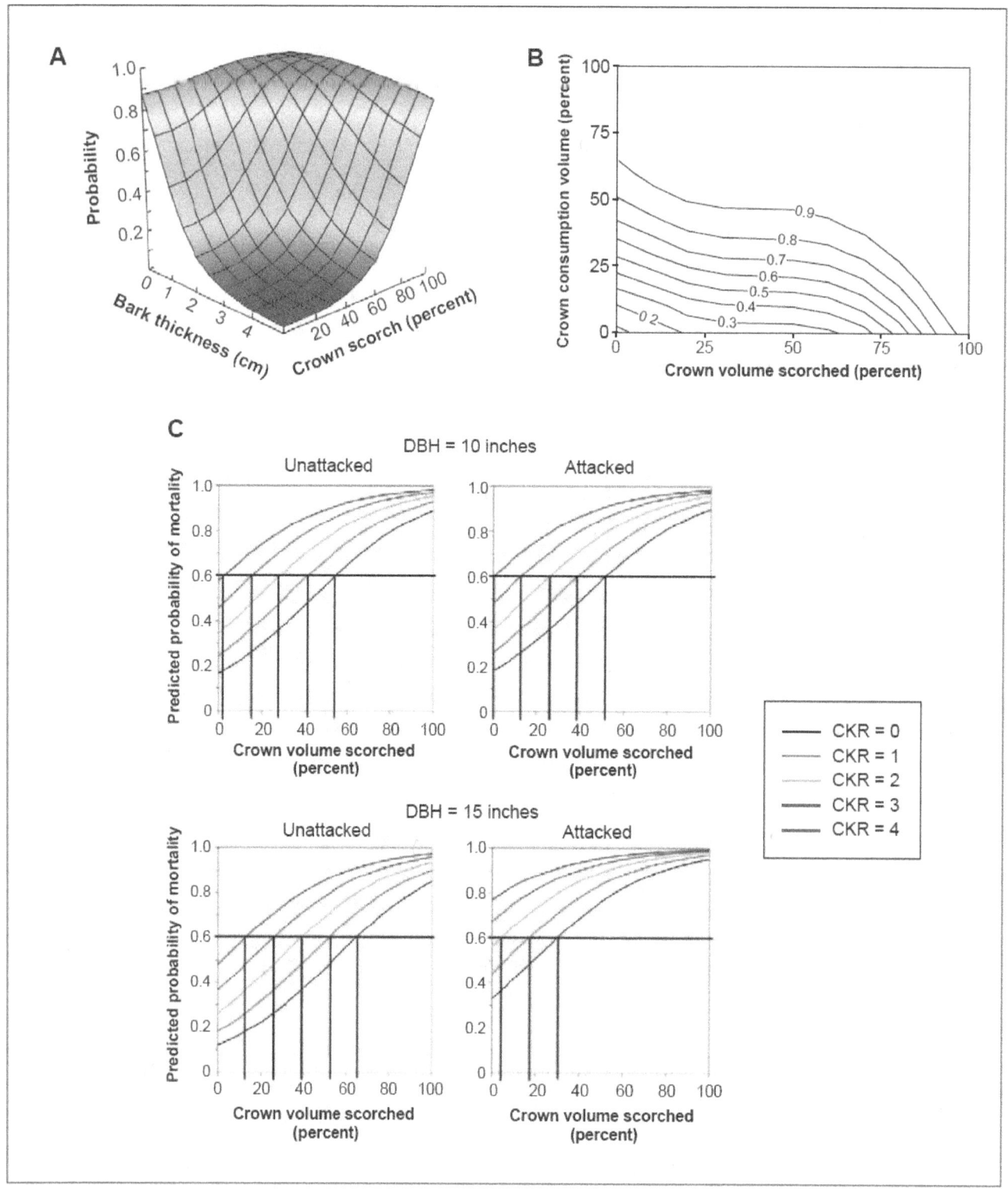

Figure 2—Probability of mortality models (A) for seven western conifers as a function of crown scorch and bark thickness (Ryan and Amman 1994), (B) crown scorch and crown consumption (Sieg et al. 2006), and (C) using crown scorch and cambium kill ratio (Hood et al. 2007). CKR = cambium kill rating (number of tree quadrants with dead cambium at ground level).

Adding another two variables, diameter at breast height (d.b.h.) and the presence of *Ips* beetles, increases accuracy even further. McHugh and colleagues (2003) found that following fire in northern Arizona ponderosa pine stands, trees having greater crown damage were preferred by *Dendroctonous* and *Ips* beetles. Burn intensity and its relationship to bark beetle attack was reported in Gibson and Negrón (2009). The Sieg and colleagues (2006) paper also has a good discussion of other postfire tree mortality studies.

Another model predicts postfire mortality in ponderosa pines in Oregon's Blue Mountains (Thies et al. 2006). This model uses easy-to-measure features, such as percentage of crown scorch and scorch height on the bole, to determine the probability of mortality. As of spring 2007, additional field testing of the model was underway. Information on the model so far is available at http://www.fs.fed.us/pnw/sciencef/scifi81.pdf.

Fowler and Sieg (2004) reviewed methods used to predict postfire mortality of ponderosa pines and Douglas-firs. Their review found that for both species, crown scorch volume was the best single predictor of mortality and also the easiest predictor to measure. Bole damage is also an important variable. Root damage is more difficult to measure, although ground char may help for estimating fire damage to roots. Connaughton (1936) mentioned heat damage to root systems causing a 1- to 2-year delayed mortality but does not provide models.

For some tree species, little research is available on postfire mortality. One study of white fir mortality in the Sierra Nevada Range found that including prefire tree vigor, measured by growth rate, along with crown scorch, improved the accuracy of postfire mortality predictions for this species (van Mantgem et al. 2003).

Peterson (1983) developed a model to estimate probability of postfire tree mortality for the Rocky Mountain region. The model predicts mortality based on crown scorch, scorch height, and bark thickness (the bark-thickness factor differentiates tree species). A 1985 study by Peterson found that crown scorch volume may be a better predictor of tree mortality than scorch height.

Planning active management in disturbed stands should address delayed mortality. In most of the models reported in the literature, crown scorch volume was a common significant variable.

Types of Changes in the Wood of Dead Conifers

Many changes occur in the wood of dead conifers. The visible changes on the outside of the tree may not have much effect—immediately—on the soundness of the wood. Fire, weather, insects, and decay fungi interact in many ways after tree death (Hadfield and Magelssen 2006, Lowell et al. 1992, Parker et al. 2006). The type of change and rate of change differ by tree species (Hadfield and Magelssen 2006, Lowell et al. 1992), these species-specific differences are discussed in the next section. Volume and value losses occur as a result of change, and the ability to use dead and dying trees in products is influenced by type of change.

"Deterioration" is damage and "decay" is decomposition.

The terms "deterioration" and "decay" have specific meanings in the discussion of wood in dead trees. Deterioration describes damages from fire, insects, or weather, such as charring, insect holes and tunnels, and cracking (weather checking). Kimmey and Furniss (1943) used the term "limited deterioration" to describe changes such as blue stain that affect the character of wood and thus reduce the value, but do not significantly impact mechanical properties of the wood or reduce the volume suitable for products. Decay describes the decomposition of wood by fungi and bacteria. Changes in the color and texture of wood are visual clues to decay, which negatively impacts the mechanical properties of wood. Incipient decay is not visible, yet measurable losses in mechanical properties may already have occurred (Wilcox 1978). Visible signs indicative of decay include conks, which may appear on the bole of the tree as early as the second year following death (fig. 3).

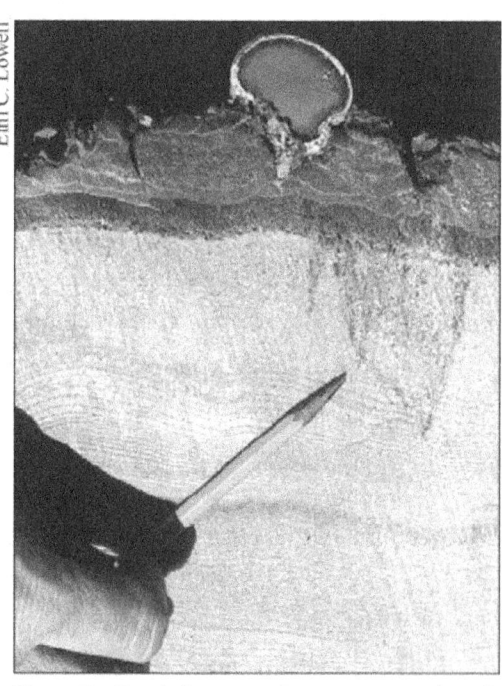

Figure 3—Pouch fungus conk on a cross section of 2-year-dead Douglas-fir log and associated sap rot.

Char—

Studies find that even when tree needles and small branches are burned and the bark charred, most wood in the bole is still sound (Hadfield and Magelssen 2006, Lowell et al. 1992). In mature and large conifers, very little wood actually burns during the fire, unless prefire injuries had exposed wood (Beal et al. 1935, Lowell et al. 1992). More of the bole wood may burn in smaller trees. Thin-barked species end up with more char on wood than thick-barked species. In eastern Washington, the char on fire-killed trees showed clear species differences (table 1). Regardless of the number of trees with char, corresponding volume loss was minimal. Fire intensity can also affect the amount of char. Figure 4 shows a lodgepole pine (thin-barked species) with (a) only bark charred, (b) char present in knots, and (c) char present in wood.

Table 1—Percentage of trees containing char and volume loss to char, by species

Tree species	Trees with char	Char volume	
		All trees	Charred trees only
		------------ *Percent* -------------	
Ponderosa pine	5.0	0.01	0.15
Western larch	5.6	0.01	0.10
Douglas-fir	6.1	0.01	0.12
Grand fir	9.9	0.02	0.19
Lodgepole pine	16.0	0.02	0.17
Engelmann spruce	19.2	0.01	0.08
Subalpine fir	38.6	0.10	0.21

Source: Hadfield and Magelssen 2006.

Figure 4—Limited char depth on lodgepole pine, a thin-barked tree species.

Weather check, cracking, and breakage—
As dead trees lose moisture, the wood shrinks and splits. Small cracks are called weather checks. Cracks start in the outer sapwood and gradually extend farther inward, allowing fungi to enter. When the bark loosens and sloughs off (fig. 5), however, the wood may dry out enough to slow or stop fungal decay. The extent of cracking (fig. 6) and the effects of cracking are influenced by several factors that are covered in the section "Factors Influencing Rate of Change."

Some trees lose enough moisture to slow or stop decay.

13

Figure 5—Loose and sloughing bark on a beetle-killed tree.

Figure 6—Weather checking in (A) standing trees (beetle-killed lodgepole pine), (B) logs (beetle-killed lutz spruce), and (C) cross section (fire-killed ponderosa pine).

Felling breakage—
More felling breakage occurs in fire-killed trees (fig. 7) than in green trees (Lowell et al. 1992). Felling breakage is more common in the upper bole. In 1- to 3-year-old fire-killed Douglas-fir, felling breakage was 18 percent, compared to 8 percent in green timber (Beal et al. 1935). Parry and colleagues (1996) found that breakage

Figure 7—Truck damage caused by tree breakage in 3-year-dead fire-killed stand of trees above.

during felling and skidding accounted for less than 4 percent volume loss in beetle-killed Douglas-fir. In another study, the felling breakage in various mixed, fire-killed stands averaged 12 percent when felling was done 3 years postfire, and 21 percent when felling was done 4 years postfire (Wallis et al. 1974).

Insect damage and stain and decay fungi—
Several major groups of insects attack stressed, weakened, damaged, or dead trees, with each group damaging trees in different ways and at different times. Insects also have complex interactions with stain and decay fungi. Following are discussions of these topics under separate headings.

Insect Damage to Conifers

The major groups of tree-attacking insects have specific preferences for live (damaged, stressed, or weakened) or dead trees and for specific parts of the tree, such as phloem, sapwood, and heartwood. For example, fire-damaged and recently dead trees attract sapwood-inhabiting insects such as ambrosia beetles. Roundheaded and flatheaded woodborers prefer trees that have been killed, whereas bark beetles generally attack weakened trees (Parker et al. 2006).

The time of year a fire occurs also plays a role in insect activity level. McHugh and colleagues (2003) found the most bark beetle activity following spring fires and less activity following autumn fires in ponderosa pine. Fire severity also influences beetle activity Richmond and Lejeune (1945) found no beetle attacks in severely burned spruce stands where the cambium had been destroyed. Not all fire-killed or fire-damaged stands will experience insect attack (Gibson and Negrón 2009, Lowell and Cahill 1996). Historically, the life cycle of many bark beetles is 1 year, whereas for roundheaded and flatheaded woodborers, the larval stage ranges from 1 to 4 years (Goheen and Willhite 2006). Insect populations are sensitive to environmental changes that could alter their life cycle, especially climate change (Lundquist and Bentz 2009).

Three main groups of insects attack fire-damaged, fire-stressed, or recently killed trees. Each group of insects has many individual species, which may have preferences for particular tree species.

Bark beetles—

Bark beetles are attracted to fire-damaged or drought-stressed trees, and they generally attack trees from late spring through early summer (Fowler and Sieg 2004, Lowell et al. 1992, Parker et al. 2006, Thies et al. 2001). In the case of fire-damaged trees, bark beetles usually attack the season after the fire. Two exceptions are known: (1) when fires are early in the season, beetles may attack the same summer and (2) fir engravers sometimes move into grand firs within weeks after a fire (Hadfield and Magelssen 2006, Lowell et al. 1992). Generally, though, managers have a window of 9 to 12 months after a fire to consider and implement their options, before bark beetles attack.

Bark beetles need enough undamaged inner bark for their larvae to eat; the larvae cannot survive in dry or fermented wood tissues (Hadfield and Magelssen 2006, Lowell et al. 1992). Therefore bark beetles will not attack severely burned stands where all cambium was destroyed, and they avoid trees dead for more than 1 year because their larvae cannot survive in the dry tissues (Hadfield and Magelssen 2006, Lowell et al. 1992). In thick-barked trees, wood borers can kill much of the cambium before bark beetles attack, reducing the food supply for bark beetle larvae and thus minimizing bark beetle attack (Furniss and Carolin 1977).

The adult bark beetles chew galleries between the bark and wood, and then lay eggs in the galleries. Their larvae tunnel inside the bark, cambium, and outer layers of sapwood, eating the fresh phloem and cambium tissues (Furniss and Carolin 1977, Parker et al. 2006). The bark beetle larvae stay in the cambium layers just under the bark, never penetrating deeper into the tree.

Several changes result from bark beetle attacks. Larval feeding loosens the tree bark, galleries are created in the outer layers of the tree, and stain and decay fungi gain entry into the tree, especially the pouch fungus (Hadfield and Magelssen 2006).

Bark beetles can build up populations large enough to kill fire-weakened trees. When the weakened trees die, bark beetles swarm to nearby live, healthy trees and attack them, weakening or killing them. Thus, over the first several years after a fire, bark beetle attack may extend the area of dead trees beyond the original fire perimeter.

There are two main genera of bark beetles associated with fire-killed trees: *Dendroctonus* and *Ips*. Each genus has many species. The *Ips* beetles attack pine and spruce and are second to *Dendroctonus* beetles in terms of destructiveness. According to Furniss and Carolin (1977), the most destructive *Dendroctonus* bark beetles are:

- Douglas-fir bark beetle—attacks Douglas-firs.
- Western pine beetle—attacks ponderosa pines.
- Mountain pine beetle—attacks ponderosa, western white, white bark, and sugar pines.
- Spruce beetle—attacks spruces.

Ambrosia beetles—

Ambrosia beetles attack recently dead or weakened trees (Kimmey and Furniss 1943, Lowell et al. 1992, Parker et al. 2006). Most ambrosia beetle attacks occur the spring after a fire, with some new attacks in the second year after a fire (Hadfield and Magelssen 2006). Ambrosia beetles, also called pinhole borers, are often the first insect to attack fire-killed trees.

Ambrosia beetles inhabit the sapwood; they generally prefer Douglas-fir, western hemlock, spruce, and true firs (Lowell et al. 1992). Their presence can be identified by the small piles of white wood dust they produce when boring into trees. The adult beetles chew tunnels about 1/16 inch in diameter, up to 3 inches deep, and then lay their eggs in the tunnels. The ambrosia beetles introduce a symbiotic fungus into the tunnels, which the larvae feed on (Furniss and Carolin 1977). The beetles also introduce other rot and stain fungi (Carpenter et al. 1988) including a fungus that causes a black to deep purple stain around the tunnels and pinhole entry points. Eglitis[4] found ambrosia beetles to be more common west of the Cascade Mountains in Oregon. On the east side of the mountains, they generally prefer true fir. The beetles will also attack ponderosa pine, but other species are rarely host to the beetle.

---

[4] Eglitis, A. 2009. Personal communication. Entomologist, Deschutes National Forest, 1001 SW Emkay Drive, Bend, OR 97702.

Wood borers

The first wood borers attack dead trees within weeks after a fire. They prefer thick-barked tree species, likely because the thick bark protects phloem and cambium tissues from fire heat, and thus these tissues are still able to support wood-borer larvae (Hadfield and Magelssen 2006, Lowell et al. 1992, Parker et al. 2006). Unlike bark beetles, wood borers generally do not build large populations that attack nearby live trees (Parker et al. 2006).

In eastern Washington, Hadfield and Magelssen (2006) found wood borer holes to be most common in Douglas-fir, western larch, ponderosa pine, and large-diameter grand fir. Wood borer holes were less common in the thin-barked tree species: subalpine fir, lodgepole pine, and Engelmann spruce. The wood borers generally abandoned the thin-barked trees after the first year, but continued to attack thick-barked Douglas-firs and ponderosa pines through the third year. However, in central Oregon, lodgepole pine is very heavily colonized by wood borers following fire (see footnote 4).

Wood borer larvae first feed in the cambium layer and then continue into the sapwood with some extending their tunnels into the heartwood (Carolin and Furniss 1977, Parker et al. 2006) as shown in figure 8. The first wood borer species to attack dead trees will disappear as the wood becomes dryer, only to be replaced by a different group of species that prefers the dry wood (Parker et al. 2006). The holes of wood borers are almost always followed by stain, caused by fungi that gain entry through wood borer holes (Hadfield and Magelssen 2006). Wood borer tunnels into sapwood and heartwood eventually become the centers of small spots of decay (Hadfield and Magelssen 2006, Lowell et al. 1992).

Figure 8—Roundheaded borer gallery (and blue stain) 2 years after Hash Rock Fire, Ochoco National Forest, Oregon (September 2002).

Sapwood-feeding wood borers include the flatheaded or metallic wood borers (family Buprestidae), roundheaded borers or long-horned beetles (family Cerambycidae), and horntails or wood wasps (family Siricidae) (DeNitto et al. 2000, Lowell et al. 1992, McCullough et al. 1998, Parker et al. 2006). The most common heartwood-feeding wood borers are various roundheaded borer species (Parker et al. 2006). Some flathead or metallic wood borers are also heartwood feeders (Parker et al. 2006). Many heartwood borers work through the sapwood and then mine the heartwood. These insects can cause great damage to the wood value of dead trees as they advance through the heartwood ahead of rot (Wright and Harvey 1967). Heartwood borers can continue their boring even after trees are felled and logs are milled, increasing the value lost.

There are a number of other insect interaction factors that can alter deterioration patterns. For example, on a dry site, insect attack can slow the rate of decay because the sapwood dries faster as the insects loosen tree bark and the bark drops off. In other cases, insect attack can accelerate decay by introducing fungi. Trees with the most infestation tend to decay faster than less infested trees of the same species and size, under similar site conditions (Lowell et al. 1992). The ponderosa borer often attacks western-pine-beetle-killed trees at the base, which can hasten falldown (Goheen and Wilhite 2006). Woodpeckers chip away at trees as they forage for beetle larvae. The woodpecker holes do not destroy much wood volume, but do cause the bark to loosen so that the trees lose moisture more rapidly (fig. 9), leading to more cracking and decay as sapwood is exposed to wind, air, and fungal spores (Hadfield and Magelssen 2006). It has also been suggested that woodpecker beaks can introduce fungal spores into trees.

Insect damage typically lowers wood value, not volume. Wood borer holes, ambrosia beetle tunnels, and bark beetle galleries lower the product grade but do not render the wood unusable (Lowell and Parry 2007, Lowell et al. 1992). The different groups of insects also host different fungi species, which then have different effects on wood quality—stains of various colors, different types of decay, and so forth (Hadfield and Magelssen 2006, Lowell et al. 1992, Parker et al. 2006). For example, bark beetles and engraver beetles inoculate trees with fungi species that differ from those introduced by ambrosia beetles and wood borers.

> **Interactions among agents can alter deterioration and decay patterns.**

Erni C. Lowell

Figure 9—Woodpecker damage in beetle-killed spruce tree in Alaska.

Stain and Decay Fungi Damage to Conifers

Stain in conifers causes little structural damage.

The spores of stain and decay fungi cannot penetrate tree bark. Fungi spores get into trees through insect bore holes, weather checks, cracks, broken branches or broken tops, and often are carried in on the bodies of insects (Aho and Cahill 1984, Hadfield and Magelssen 2006, Lowell et al. 1992). Heartrot decay fungi may be present in trees from previous wounds or get into trees through fire-scarred roots (Littke and Gara 1986, Lowell et al. 1992).

Insects, fire, and fungi interact in many ways in western conifer forests (Lowell et al. 1992, Parker et al. 2006). Trees that already have root rot and heart rot before fires may be more susceptible, after fire damage, to other types of decay or beetle attacks (Parker et al. 2006). Also, the rot-infected trees may be sources of fungi spores, carried by insects to weakened and damaged trees (Parker et al. 2006). Other interactions among insects and fungi are discussed throughout this section.

Factors affecting the rate of decay—

In general, the rate of decay is influenced by temperature, moisture, and oxygen (Aho and Cahill 1984, Lowell et al. 1992). Few decay fungi can survive in wood with less than 20 percent moisture content. Wood decay fungi grow best at temperatures between 27 and 33 °C (Cartwright and Findlay 1958). Therefore, dead trees on dry, south or west slopes at high elevations may be slower to decay than dead trees on moist, north or east slopes at low elevations. However, the same factors that slow decay may result in more weather checking or cracking in dead trees.

Moisture differences between maritime climates and interior western climates affect decay rates. Parry and colleagues (1996) found only pouch fungus conks in their 4-year study of tree decay in northeastern Oregon, but Wright and Wright (1954) found red belt fungus conks on trees dead for 2 or more years in the moister climate of coastal Oregon and Washington.

Although fungi cause both stains and decay, the types of damage are quite different (Hadfield and Magelssen 2006, Lowell et al. 1992). Stains change the color of the wood but do not weaken the wood or reduce the volume. Decay occurs when fungi or bacteria species break down wood cell walls.

Stain—

In the first year after a fire, stain is the most important form of fungus-caused deterioration (Hadfield and Magelssen 2006, Lowell et al. 1992). Most staining occurs in the sapwood, which has more moisture and sugars than the heartwood.

Blue stain fungi, the most common group of sapwood-staining fungi species, appear in susceptible trees (i.e., thick-barked species with large sapwood volume that were not severely burned) within 1 year after a fire (Lowell et al. 1992). The spores of blue stain fungi are introduced mostly by bark beetles but sometimes by wood borers (Hadfield and Magelssen 2006, Lowell et al. 1992).

Susceptibility to blue stain differs by tree species. Under the right conditions, blue stain fungi spread rapidly in the radial and longitudinal direction (Parmeter et al. 1992). Conditions favorable for blue stain fungi are also favorable for other fungi, so blue stain in sapwood is an early sign that decay fungi may be present. By the third year after tree death, sapwood decay becomes the primary reason for the deterioration of wood quality, overriding any concerns about stain discoloration (Lowell et al. 1992).

Other stains also affect dead conifers. Ambrosia beetle pinholes and galleries are often stained dark brown or black. Other stains may discolor the heartwood, but these generally fade with drying (Kimmey 1955). The fir engraver is associated with the stain fungus *Trichosporium symbioticum* (no common name) (Parry et al. 1996).

Stain in conifers causes little structural damage, although a loss in one mechanical property, toughness, can occur. However, the change in appearance of products can result in a lower lumber grade, and thus value loss. The value loss is greater for species with a high proportion of sapwood, such as pines, or when appearance grade products, such as Select, Moulding, and Shop grades, are produced (Lowell et al. 1992). Figure 10 illustrates blue stain from the tree to the product.

Decay—

Sapwood in all conifer species is susceptible to decay by insects and fungi (Panshin and deZeeuw 1964). It is the first merchantable wood in fire-killed or -damaged trees to be attacked by insects and stain and decay fungi (Lowell et al. 1992). Once decay fungi are established, they will, under the right conditions, continue to deteriorate the wood even after the tree is cut. Decay decreases the mechanical properties of wood as it destroys the cell walls. Losses can be measurable even when the loss of weight (volume loss) is small (Kennedy 1958, Wilcox 1978). Weakened, decayed wood may be unsuitable for structural

Figure 10—Blue stain in fire-killed ponderosa pine (A) tree, 3 months following fire, (B) end of a log, (C) sawn cant, and (D) side of lumber stack.

lumber. Smith and colleagues (1987) found a reduction in some mechanical properties after 3 years when looking at decay in peeled, air-dried Douglas-fir poles.

Sapwood decays faster than heartwood, so trees with larger proportions of sapwood (i.e., fir species and western hemlock) are more prone to decay; trees with larger proportions of heartwood (i.e., larches, Douglas-fir, and old growth of most conifer species) resist decay (Aho and Cahill 1984). Young trees that have not yet formed much heartwood will decay more quickly than older trees. Likewise, small-diameter trees generally decay faster than large-diameter trees. However, trees that grew rapidly and thus have a large proportion of sapwood may decay at rates comparable to small-diameter trees (Lowell et al. 1992). When studying Douglas-fir logs from felled trees, Smith and colleagues (1970) found increased decay rates with decreasing log size and increasing sapwood proportion. Some fungi (e.g., *Fomitopsis pinicola*) in the sapwood may also extend decay into the heartwood (Smith et al. 1970).

The first stages of decay do not always discolor the wood, and the fungi hyphae may extend beyond any discoloration that is present (Kimmey and Furniss 1943). Conks, or sporophores, on standing trees are definite indicators of decay fungi in the wood. Visual clues of decay, such as stain, advanced decay, fiber-pulling in springwood, and soft springwood, may not be sufficient to detect all decay in structural lumber.

Most (80 percent) of Douglas-fir beetles carry decay fungi such as red belt fungus, pouch fungus, and others (Harrington et al. 1981). The text box on the next page describes some important decay fungi. Bark beetles can also bring in root rot fungi, which do not affect wood quality directly but may kill the tree eventually.

Rate of change from decay fungi—
Generally, little wood volume is lost to decay within the first year after a fire (Hadfield and Magelssen 2006). Pouch fungus, associated with rot in the outer sapwood, is often found after 1 year in beetle-killed trees (Wright and Wright 1954). Although it often appears in abundance, the decay associated with it is minimal.

By the second year after the fire, sapwood rot becomes an important factor in the deterioration of fire-killed timber (Lowell et al. 1992). Red belt fungus becomes common in trees dead 2 or more years, indicating more advanced decay, often with much sapwood destroyed and perhaps invasion of heartwood (Wright and Wright 1954). For some conifer species under some conditions, most sapwood was no longer usable after 3 years (Beal et al. 1935, Kimmey 1955). However, in eastern Washington, Hadfield and Magelssen (2006) found that the volume of decayed wood increased only slightly in the second and third years after a fire, with total wood volume lost low.

Important Decay Fungi for Conifers in the Western United States

Pouch fungus (*Cryptoporus volvatus*). This sapwood decayer causes gray-brown saprot (actually appears as a thick, white mycelium) (Parker et al. 2006). In fire- and beetle-killed trees, the conks may appear as soon as 1 year after tree death, and they may also grow on weakened trees. The conks, referred to as "popcorn conks," are globular sporophores that protrude from insect holes in the bark (Hayashi et al. 1996). The conks dry out and fall off in 2 to 3 years (Wright and Harvey 1967). The fungus produces a light tan discoloration that is difficult to detect on the end surface of a log. Douglas-fir beetle and wood borer infestations carry pouch fungus into trees, where it grows quickly in the moist, sugar-rich phloem and cambium (Hadfield and Magelssen 2006). Spores may also be disseminated aerially.

Quinine fungus (*Fomitopsis officinalis*). This fungus decays both sapwood and heartwood and shows as yellow or pink to light reddish brown discoloration. It is more common in older burns (Kimmey and Furniss 1943).

Red belt fungus (*Fomitopsis pinicola*). This sapwood and heartwood fungus gets in either through deep wood borer holes or decayed sapwood (Parker et al. 2006). During early stages in sapwood, the fungus appears as a pale yellow to light brown discoloration. As decay advances, the red belt fungus causes a brown, crumbly rot. Red belt conks are common on beetle-killed trees dead for 2 years or more. Presence of these conks indicates unsound sapwood and the possibility of decaying heartwood (Wright and Wright 1954).

Artist's conk (*Ganoderma applanatum*). This fungus is active only in the sapwood of the butt log. It appears as a tan to brown, sometimes purplish brown to violet stain. It can be an important decay fungus for hemlock, but it has exacting moisture require-ments and is generally not important for fire-killed trees of other species.

No common name (*Gloeophyllum sepiarium*). This fungus is a brown rot that rapidly destroys the sapwood and also works in the heartwood. It causes pale tan to brown patches of discoloration and is found more often on drier sites. Brown rot destroys the cellulose and hemicellulose and decreases pulp yield (Wallis et al. 1974, Wright et al. 1956).

Purple fungus (*Trichaptum abietinum*). The purple fungus causes a white rot respon-sible for the majority of sapwood deterioration in fire-killed Douglas-fir. The light yellow to tan discoloration appears the first or second year after the fire. Conks may appear 2 to 5 years after the tree is dead (Parker et al. 2006).

By the fourth year after a fire, decay may extend into the heartwood (Lowell et al. 1992). However, the extent of decay may differ at different levels up and down the bole, and even at different areas around the circumference. Grand fir, ponderosa pine, and Douglas-fir lost the most wood volume to decay over 5 years (Hadfield and Magelssen 2006). Thin-barked species (subalpine fir, lodgepole pine, Engelmann spruce, and western larch) lost very little volume to decay, even after 5 years (Hadfield and Magelssen 2006). The two species of fungi most associated with saprot in 5-year-dead Douglas-fir in interior British Columbia were the red belt and purple fungi (Thomas and Craig 1958).

Factors Influencing the Rate of Deterioration

Many factors affect the rate of wood deterioration, including, but not limited to, the tree species, cause of tree death (insect, fire, or wind), precipitation, aspect, and elevation (Lowell et al. 1992).

Tree species influences rate of deterioration.

Tree species—

The tree species is the most important factor affecting the rate of deterioration, and bark thickness is the most important species characteristic related to deterioration (Lowell et al. 1992). Within-tree variation that affects rate of change is illustrated in figure 11.

Moving up the bole:
- Diameter decreases
- Sapwood proportion increases
- Age decreases
- Bark thickness decreases
- Ring width increases

Figure 11—Relationship of within-tree characteristics that influence deterioration and decay, by vertical position.

Bark thickness—

Thin-barked and thick-barked tree species differ as to whether basal logs or upper logs crack first (Hadfield and Magelssen 2006). Also, loose bark, such as bark loosened by bark beetle tunneling or woodpeckers, increases cracking in the sapwood.

- **Thin-barked species (Englemann spruce, lodgepole pine, subalpine fir, grand fir, western white pine, western larch):** Thin-barked species crack more quickly and extensively within the first year than thick-barked species (Hadfield and Magelssen 2006). In thin-barked species, basal logs develop cracks more quickly than upper logs (Hadfield and Magelssen 2006). Thin-barked species stood longer as snags than thick-barked species in eastern Washington (Everett et al. 1999). On thin-barked tree species (grand fir, subalpine fir, lodgepole pine, Engelmann spruce), bark below the snow level sloughed off trees sooner than bark above snow level (Lowell et al. 1992). Where bark was lost because of the snow, cracks formed sooner. The wood of thin-barked species (i.e., lodgepole pine, western white pine, small-diameter firs, and Engelmann spruce) tends to dry quickly, and the lack of moisture impedes fungi growth. Because their wood dries faster, the thin-barked species are more susceptible to cracking.

- **Thick-barked species (Douglas-fir, grand fir, ponderosa pine):** Thick bark tends to delay cracking by 1 year. The basal log is the least likely to crack in the first 2 years. As wood borers and bark beetles loosened bark, thick-barked trees developed cracks even though the trees retained most of their bark (Hadfield and Magelssen 2006, Lowell et al. 1992). The wood of thick-barked species (i.e., Douglas-fir, ponderosa pine, and large, old grand fir) and trees grown in moist conditions (i.e., west of the Cascade Range crest or riparian areas) retain more moisture and are less prone to cracking but more susceptible to decay fungi. Western larch is one exception to this trend; although it has thick bark, it is very resistant to decay (Hadfield and Magelssen 2006).

Proportion of sapwood to heartwood—

Sapwood holds more moisture and contains fewer anti-fungal substances than heartwood, so it decays more rapidly than heartwood (Aho and Cahill 1984, Lowell et al. 1992). The proportion of sapwood to heartwood, which is a function of species and age, is the second most important characteristic after tree species influencing the rate of deterioration (Lowell et al. 1992). Tree species with a higher proportion of sapwood, such as western hemlock and Pacific silver fir, deteriorate faster than tree species with a lower proportion of sapwood. Younger trees, with a high proportion of sapwood, generally deteriorate more rapidly than older trees (Lowell et al. 1992).

Heartwood decay rates differ among species. Aho and Cahill (1984) found that west of the Cascade Range crest in Oregon, western hemlock and Pacific silver fir heartwood deteriorated the fastest, followed by Douglas-fir, and then western redcedar.

Diameter of trees or logs—

Small-diameter logs usually deteriorate faster than large-diameter logs, and upper logs deteriorate faster than basal logs, again because of the greater proportion of sapwood (Aho and Cahill 1984, Lowell et al. 1992). If a tree is large because it grew rapidly, its decay rate may be similar to the rate for a smaller tree. Conversely, if a tree is small because it has suppressed growth, then the decay may be slower.

Cracks (fig. 6) in small-diameter logs or small-diameter sections of the tree bole allow wood to dry faster, making it less susceptible to insects and fungi. Small-diameter trees break sooner than large trees. In large-diameter trees or large-diameter sections of the tree bole, cracks may not cause drying but simply allow stain and decay to enter the tree (Hadfield and Magelssen 2006, Lowell et al. 1992).

Rate of growth—

Trees that grow rapidly decay more quickly than trees that grow slowly (Lowell et al. 1992). The rate of growth, or width of the annual rings, influences the deterioration rate in both the sapwood and heartwood of conifers. Rapidly grown heartwood deteriorates more rapidly in the radial direction than slower grown heartwood.

Position of wood in the stem—

The upper portions of a tree bole are smaller in diameter and have a larger proportion of sapwood to heartwood than the lower bole (fig. 11). Thus the middle portions of a dead tree generally contain more decay proportionately than the basal logs (Lowell et al. 1992). The bark also gets thinner as you move toward the top of the bole: thus the upper bole often cracks more quickly because it dries more quickly (but see thin-barked tree species, above) (Lowell et al. 1992). Deeply cracked upper logs are generally very dry and thus have very little decay and few wood borer holes. However, when tops begin to break off dead trees, decay fungi can enter the exposed wood of the broken top (Lowell et al. 1992).

Species of insects and fungi present—
Insect activity is usually the mechanism that introduces stain and decay fungi (Lowell et al. 1992). Once decay enters the bole, it will deteriorate the sapwood ahead of insect damage (Kimmey and Furniss 1943, Wright and Harvey 1967).

Site characteristics—
Fungi and insects require certain levels of moisture, temperature, and oxygen to establish themselves and to thrive. Excessive moisture or extreme dryness can limit or stop deterioration (Lowell et al. 1992). On moist sites (i.e., riparian areas and stands west of the Cascade Range crest) severely burned trees may decay faster than less severely burned trees. But in dry forests (east of the Cascade Range crest, and interior Western States) the opposite is true, because these trees may be too dry to support insect larvae and decay fungi (Lowell et al. 1992). Aspect, elevation, and slope position also influence moisture and temperature. Trees on hot, dry, or windy sites generally crack more quickly than those on cooler, moister sites (Hadfield and Magelssen 2006, Lowell et al. 1992).

Weather—
Dry, hot summers and low humidity result in more drying and wood shrinkage, and thus more weather checking. The faster wood dries, the more cracking occurs (Hadfield and Magelssen 2006, Lowell et al. 1992). Wind is also influential in drying rate.

Stand history—
Preexisting damage or disease in the stand, stand density, and drought are factors that can affect the rate of deterioration (Lowell et al. 1992).

Species-Specific Changes in Wood Quality of Dead and Dying Conifers

Western conifers are well-known for their distinctive characters—the thick, cinnamon-colored bark of ponderosa pine; strong, fast-growing wood of Douglas-fir; snow-hardiness and spire shape of subalpine fir; and so forth. These characteristics continue to have ecological implications when trees are dying or dead. For example, some western conifer species are more decay-resistant and stand longer as snags, which may make snags of these species more desirable for wildlife trees. Some species are attacked more heavily by wood-boring insects than other species, which has implications for woodpeckers and other insect-eating birds.

These tree species differences have economic implications as well. Decay resistance, susceptibility to stain, and degree of insect attack can affect postfire

Decay affects the mechanical properties of wood.

salvage values. Stain and bark beetle galleries affect mainly the appearance, and not the mechanical properties, of wood, but these aesthetic changes can still reduce the value of wood. Decay affects the mechanical properties of wood and can result in a significant loss of value.

This section summarizes the current knowledge about deterioration rates and other postdeath changes for the main tree species affected by various disturbance agents. Extensive data are available for five species or species groups enabling us to provide summary tables of how effects evolve during the first 5 years of the postdisturbance period (Boyce 1929, Hadfield and Magelssen 2006, Kimmey and Furniss 1943, Lowell et al. 1992, Parker et al. 2006, Wallis et al. 1974). The discussions of volume in this section and in the tables refer to the volume of standing timber. Potential product loss will be discussed in the next section. As discussed in the previous sections, variations in regional climate and study methods have resulted in some variation in deterioration rates reported in the literature. We include results from more than one publication to show the range of findings.

Douglas-Fir (*Pseudotsuga menziesii*)

There are extensive studies of postdisturbance changes in Douglas-fir as summarized in table 2. In general, the thick bark and a low proportion of sapwood in Douglas-fir protects the wood from drying, making it one of the least susceptible species to cracking and weather check. However, the moist wood is attractive to wood borers, and, along with western larch, Douglas-fir is one of the species most heavily attacked by wood borers. Woodpeckers drill for the wood borers. Fire-weakened Douglas-firs, including mature trees with only moderate crown scorch, are often attacked by Douglas-fir beetles. The beetles may kill trees that survived fires, and as the beetles exhaust this food supply, they often later attack nearby unscorched trees.

Douglas-fir bark can be tenacious, with little bark dropping in the first 5 years after death. With bark holding in wood moisture and insects bringing in pouch, red belt, and purple fungi spores, small spots of sapwood decay appear by the second year after death. Conks appear in 2 to 5 years after the tree is dead. The upper parts of the tree bole decay faster than the basal logs. By the fourth year, deterioration can begin to reach the heartwood. In the fifth year, much of the sapwood has decayed and some decay is reaching the heartwood. The ponderous wood borer attacks Douglas-firs 5 to 8 years after death, when sapwood is decayed.

Volume loss is minimal in the first 2 years but can increase starting in the third year, depending on the extent of weather cracking, insects, and decay. By the fifth year, tree breakage is more common along with branch loss.

Table 2—Douglas-fir 5-year timeline of postdisturbance changes

	Year 1	Year 2	Year 3	Year 4	Year 5
Insect activity	Wood borers infest the sapwood of most trees. Douglas-fir engravers penetrate thin, uncharred bark, and Douglas-fir beetles attack scorched trees. Woodpeckers drill after the insects.	Wood borer larvae are common, and woodpeckers drill in pursuit of the insect larvae.	Past activity continues.	Past activity continues.	Past activity continues.
Stain	Small stain patches appear in the outer sapwood of most trees.	Stain appears in the outer sapwood of all trees, but volume affected is still minor.	Almost all sapwood is stained.	Previously stained wood is decaying.	Stain becomes irrelevant as decay increases.
Weather check	Cracks develop in about one-third of trees but are shallow, not affecting much volume.	Although most bark remains on trees, it loosens, and cracks develop in most trees.	The number of cracks grows and cracks deepen.	Cracks continue to affect about one-third of volume.	Cracks become irrelevant as decay increases.
Decay	Studies find anywhere from no decay to about 11 percent sapwood rot.	Small spots of sapwood decay are widespread, but little volume is affected yet.	About 8 percent sapwood rot.	Decay spots appear in all trees. The volume of decayed wood increases.	Almost all sapwood is decayed, especially in basal logs. Large, slow-growing Douglas-firs had less decay than smaller, faster-growing Douglas-firs. However, most heartwood was still sound.
Breakage	Minimal.	Minimal.	Tree tops begin to break.	More tree tops break.	Tree breakage is more common. Branch loss is also more common.
Volume loss	Minimal.	Cracks affected about 20 percent of volume in standing trees.	Cracks affect nearly one-third of volume. However, stained volume and cracked volume overlap each other, so the percentages are not cumulative.	Decayed wood volume ranges from 6 to 11 percent in various studies.	Not documented.

References: Beal et al. 1935, Furniss 1937, Hadfield and Magelssen 2006, Kimmey and Furniss 1943, Lowell et al. 1992, Parker et al. 2006, Parry et al. 1996, Wallis et al. 1974, Wright and Wright 1954.

Engelmann Spruce and White Spruce (*Picea engelmanii* and *Picea glauca*)

More data are available on Engelmann spruce than on white spruce, but the available data summarized in table 3 can be used for both species. Much of the available data deals with the rapid and heavy ambrosia beetle attack of Engelmann spruce. In Hadfield and Magelssen (2006), Engelmann spruce had the most ambrosia beetle galleries of all tree species in the study. Some bark beetle galleries were seen also. Engelmann and white spruce are attacked by spruce beetles, engraver beetles, flatheaded or metallic wood borers, and roundheaded borers or long-horned beetles.

Engelmann spruce are highly susceptible to cracking, which in the Hadfield and Magelssen study (2006) affected nearly 40 percent of volume by the second year after tree death. With wood drying rapidly because of the deep cracks, decay is limited in the first several years after tree death. In both Engelmann and white spruce, decay can still be minor several years after tree death. Engelmann spruce are slow to break.

Grand Fir and White Fir (*Abies grandis* and *Abies concolor*)

Table 4 summarizes various data for the true firs. Generally, these species have thin bark and a high proportion of sapwood that causes them to deteriorate more quickly than other western conifers. (Subalpine fir is an exception; see that heading for details). Some studies suggest that grand firs decayed the fastest of all species. Differences between the studies (Hadfield and Magelssen 2006, Parry et al. 1996) might be the result of different site conditions or differences in the fungi spores brought in by Douglas-fir beetles compared to the fungi spores brought in by fir engravers.

The thin bark drops off trees rapidly in the first years after tree death, allowing rapid drying and rapid cracking. Bark loss is most severe on basal logs. Initially, the rapid development of deep cracks is the primary cause of loss of usable volume in dead true firs. The rapid cracking leads next to rapid decay; the heartwood of true firs is less durable than heartwood of other western conifers. In true firs, wood decay often begins in the roots and root collars and moves up into the boles. Decay spots appear in most true firs during the first 2 years after tree death, but spots are still small. The decay increases rapidly after the second year, and by the fourth year after tree death, almost all sapwood in the basal logs of grand fir is decayed. The extent of decay leads to significant volume losses in standing trees.

Table 3—Englemann spruce and white spruce 5-year timeline of postdisturbance changes

	Year 1	Year 2	Year 3	Year 4	Year 5
Insect activity	Ambrosia beetle attack is heavy. Few wood borers attack trees, and consequently woodpecker foraging is also light.	Wood borers attack about half the trees.	Insect infestation continues but is generally light.	Insect infestation continues but is generally light.	Wood borer holes increase and the holes deepen; affecting three-fourths of trees.
Stain	All trees are likely to have stain, primarily associated with the ambrosia beetle attacks.	Sapwood stain affects about 20 percent of Englemann spruce volume.	Minimal change from year 2.	Minimal change from year 3.	About a third of Englemann spruce volume is affected by stain.
Weather check	Majority of trees are likely to crack. Cracks are most common close to the ground.	All trees are likely to have cracks.	Deep cracks can develop.	The percentage of volume affected by cracks continues to rise slowly.	The percentage of volume affected by cracks continues to rise.
Decay	Minimal.	Small spots of decay exist in about one-third of trees, affecting less than 1 percent of volume.	Small spots of decay exist but affect a minimal amount of volume.	Small spots of decay exist but affect a minimal amount of volume.	Small spots of decay, found mostly near cracks in basal logs, affect a minor amount of volume.
Breakage	Minimal.	Minimal.	Much bark is gone from basal logs, but upper logs retain most of their bark. Fine branches are dropping.	Cracks are likely to affect more than half the volume.	Basal logs lost about two-thirds of their bark, but upper logs still had about 60 percent of their bark. Tops began to break and larger branches began to drop.
Volume loss	Minimal.	Cracks affected nearly 40 percent of Englemann spruce volume.	Cracks affected about 45 percent of Englemann spruce volume.	Minimal change from year 3.	Cracks affect more than half the volume.

References: Hadfield and Magelssen 2006, Lowell et al. 1992, Parker et al. 2006.

Table 4—True fir (*Abies* spp.) 5-year timeline of postdisturbance changes

	Year 1	Year 2	Year 3	Year 4	Year 5
Insect activity	Wood borers infest most trees and already extend into sapwood. Wood-pecker foraging is common. Fir engravers infest the majority of firs, always above scorched bark, and engravers bring in pouch fungus. Ambrosia beetles also attack true firs.	Wood borers infest all trees.	Not documented.	Not documented.	Not documented.
Stain	Spots of stain are found in most or all trees, but only a small percentage of volume is affected.	Minimal change from year 1.	Stain affects about a quarter of volume.	Stain can affect one-third or more of volume.	The amount of stain is irrelevant, as decay is significant.
Weather check	Most grand firs crack in the first year.	Cracks are prevalent in all trees.	More than half of tree bark is gone, and deep cracks affect half the volume or more.	Not documented.	Not documented.
Decay	Sapwood decay is already present in over half the trees, but decay spots are small and affect little volume.	Most trees have spots of decay and many trees have pouch fungus conks. Decay spots are still small, affecting little volume.	Spots of sapwood decay are common in basal logs, but the percentage of volume affected is still minor.	Most sapwood in the basal log shows decay.	Typically, all sapwood in basal logs is decayed.
Breakage	Not documented.	Not documented.	Trees began to break. Many branches are already dropped.	Tree breakage is common. Some true firs break at the root collar because the outer wood is case-hardened.	Trees continue to break and lose most branches.
Volume loss	Checking affects about 14 percent of grand fir volume.	Cracking affects one-third or more of volume.	Cracking and decay reduces volume.	Not documented.	Nearly 40 percent of total volume in true firs was decayed.

References: Hadfield and Magelssen 2006, Kimmey 1955, Lowell et al. 1992, Parry et al. 1996, Snellgrove and Fahey 1977.

Lodgepole Pine (*Pinus contorta*)

Table 5 summarizes various data for lodgepole pine, a thin-bark species. Lodgepole pines are highly susceptible to blue stain and cracking, but can be decay resistant if their moisture content decreases rapidly. Dead lodgepole pines have fewer insect attacks than most western conifers because they are commonly found on drier sites. The most common insects to attack lodgepole are pine engravers and mountain pine beetles. Some ambrosia beetles and wood borers attack lodgepoles, but lodgepoles have fewer of these insects, and thus less woodpecker foraging, than other western conifers.

Almost all sapwood in lodgepole pine is blue stained by the end of the first year after tree death. According to Hadfield and Magelssen (2006), lodgepole had the most volume affected by stain in the first year of all tree species studied. The stain is associated with bark beetle galleries, wood borer holes, and cracks.

Table 5—Lodgepole pine 5-year timeline of postdisturbance changes

	Year 1	Year 2	Year 3	Year 4	Year 5
Insect activity	Pine engraver and mountain pine beetle galleries are common. A few wood borer holes and ambrosia beetle galleries are found.	Wood borers infest one-third or more of trees.	Not documented.	Not documented.	Not documented.
Stain	Nearly all sapwood is blue stained, affecting from one-third to two-thirds of total volume.	Typically, all sapwood is blue stained.	All sapwood is stained.	Not documented.	Not documented.
Weather check	Cracks are common, likely to affect at least half the trees.	All trees are likely to have cracks, affecting significant volume.	Cracks affect the majority of standing trees. Bark is dropping from basal logs.	Most bark is gone from basal logs.	Nearly all volume is affected by staining and cracks.
Decay	Little or none.	A few small spots of decay may exist, affecting little volume.	Decay spots are small, affecting minimal volume.	Minimal change from year 3.	Decay is minor.
Breakage	Not documented.	Not documented.	Not documented.	Not documented.	Upper logs retained about 70 percent of their bark. Little branch loss occurred in the first 4 years, but considerable branch loss occurred in year 5.
Volume loss	Minimal.	Minimal.	Cracks cause significant volume loss.	Not documented.	Almost all volume is lost because of stain and cracks.

References: Fahey et al. 1986, Hadfield and Magelssen 2006, Harvey 1979, Lowell et al. 1992, Parker et al. 2006, Snellgrove and Cahill 1980.

Because lodgepoles crack quickly, the wood is too dry for most decay fungi. The blue-stained wood typically shows little decay, even 5 years after tree death. What decay exists is usually in the basal logs, which retain some moisture and also are affected by decay spreading up from the roots and root collars. This can lead to increased fall rate (also called falldown by Goheen and Willhite 2006) (Mitchell and Preistler 1998). The dry upper parts of lodgepole boles are very decay resistant. The extensive cracking, however, can cause significant volume losses by the third year and near total loss by the fifth year.

Ponderosa, Sugar, Western White, and Jeffrey Pine (*Pinus ponderosa*, *Pinus lambertiana*, *Pinus monticola*, and *Pinus jeffreyi*)

Table 6 summarizes various data for ponderosa, sugar, western white, and Jeffrey pines. These species have a high proportion of sapwood, making up 50 to 75 percent of the tree's total volume. Bark can be medium-thick to thick. Most data are for ponderosa pines and can be generalized to the other species. Fire-damaged ponderosa pines are attacked by western pine beetle, mountain pine beetle, pine engraver, and wood borers. Bark beetles prefer ponderosas with more crown damage, but enough green phloem and live buds for their larvae to survive.

Ponderosa pines decay rapidly after tree death because of their thick bark and high proportion of sapwood. Ponderosas lose little bark in the first 5 years after tree death, and decay fungi thrive in the moist wood. The ponderosas also break quicker and the snags topple sooner than other western conifers. The cracking rate is low; Hadfield and Magelssen (2006) found ponderosa pines had the least first-year cracking of all species in their study. Blue stain shows up quickly in ponderosas, with almost all sapwood blue stained by the end of the first year after tree death. By the third year, blue-stained wood in ponderosas is decaying, and by the fourth year, most sapwood in basal logs is decayed.

Sugar pine is notable for the slow decay of its heartwood. In large, old sugar pines, 50 percent of the heartwood may still be sound 4 years after tree death. The heartwood of western white pine, in contrast, is slightly less durable than Douglas-fir heartwood. Fire-damaged Jeffrey pines are attacked by red turpentine beetles initially, and later by Jeffrey pine beetles.

Cracking starts to lead to volume losses in the first year postdisturbance. Extensive staining can be expected in the first year for ponderosa pine. By the second year, cracking accelerates and decay further increases volume losses so that by the fifth year there is little volume that has not been affected.

Table 6—Ponderosa, sugar, western white, and jeffrey pine 5-year timeline of postdisturbance changes

	Year 1	Year 2	Year 3	Year 4	Year 5
Insect activity	Wood borers infest most trees, and woodpecker foraging is common.	Wood borers infest all trees, and woodpecker foraging is common. Of the bark beetles, pine engravers are the most common, followed by western pine beetles and mountain pine beetles. The beetles bring in pouch fungus spores.	Not documented.	Wood borer holes are common, and carpenter ants appear.	Not documented.
Stain	Nearly all trees have blue stain in sapwood, affecting 25 to 50 percent of volume.	All sapwood volume is blue stained in ponderosas; most sapwood is blue stained in sugar pines.	About 75 percent of ponderosa volume is stained.	Stain becomes irrelevant as decay and cracks increase.	Stain becomes irrelevant as decay and cracks increase.
Weather check	Trees on dry sites, small trees and the top logs of bigger trees start to develop cracks.	Cracks develop in over half the trees.	Cracks are found in most trees.	All trees have cracks, but decay begins to obscure the cracks.	Not documented.
Decay	Decay spots exist in some trees; 10 percent of ponderosas had pouch fungus conks already. Sugar pine shows little decay at this point.	Decay can affect up to 50 percent of sapwood. Pouch fungus conks are becoming common. Sugar pines show insect damage or visible decay in 75 percent of their sapwood.	Decay is found in many trees. Most sapwood decayed.	Decay increases substantially; red rot conks appear on some trees.	All trees have considerable decay.
Breakage	Not documented.	Not documented.	Top breaks and bole breaks begin to occur in some trees.	More trees break, and branch loss is substantial.	More trees break.
Volume loss	Cracks affect about 16 percent of volume.	Cracks may affect one-third of volume.	Cracks affect up to one-third of volume.	Sapwood decay increases volume losses.	More than 75 percent of volume decayed.

References: Fowler and Sieg 2004, Furniss and Carolin 1977, Hadfield and Magelssen 2006, Lowell et al. 1992, Parker et al. 2006, Sieg et al. 2006, Snellgrove and Fahey 1977.

Subalpine Fir (*Abies lasiocarpa*)

Unlike other true firs, subalpine firs are very decay resistant. The thin-barked trees crack quickly and deeply, and as a result, subalpine firs are generally too dry for decay fungi to thrive. In the Hadfield and Magelssen study (2006), subalpine firs cracked the fastest of all seven species, with some cracks already reaching the center of tree boles in the first year and affecting almost 40 percent of the volume. By the end of the second year in the Hadfield and Magelssen study (2006), trees lost much of their bark, and extensive cracking affected almost 60 percent of the volume. Cracks continue to develop in subalpine firs and fine branches drop, but the decay-resistant boles generally hold up well, with minimal breakage even after 5 years.

Dead subalpine firs do not attract as many insects as other western conifers. Wood borers infested only about one-third of subalpine firs during the first year in the Hadfield and Magelssen (2006) study, and very few wood borer attacks occurred after the first year. Woodpecker drilling is minimal. Subalpine firs get some ambrosia beetles and few or no bark beetles.

Subalpine firs are resistant to fungal staining. Five years after tree death, stain is likely to affect only a minor percentage of volume, even though most trees may have some small spots of stain. Decay develops only slowly, and the small decay spots that are present often spread from the roots and root collars up into the basal logs. Very little decay is found in the dry, cracked upper portions of the tree boles. Five years after tree death, decay affects only a minor percentage of the volume, only 4 percent in the Hadfield and Magelssen study (2006).

Western Hemlock (*Tsuga heterophylla*)

Fewer data of postdisturbance changes are available on western hemlock. Because hemlock grows in moister environments, it is not often disturbed by fire. Western hemlock deteriorates more rapidly than Douglas-fir, with decay in over half the volume by the fourth year after tree death. By the fifth year, most standing trees have decay and significant volume loss.

Western Larch (*Larix occidentalis*)

Less information is available on the western larch. Western larch is rated the most fire-resistant of western conifers. After western larch are dead, the trees are very decay resistant, perhaps because they are so susceptible to cracking. About two-thirds of western larch develop cracks in the first year after tree death, although only a small percentage of volume is affected at this point. In the second year, essentially all western larch have cracks, and in the Hadfield and Magelssen study

(2006), the cracks affected nearly 40 percent of volume. Many cracks reach the center of boles by the fourth year.

Wood borers attack western larch heavily in the first year after tree death, and woodpecker foraging is also heavy. Western larch had the most wood borer holes of all species studied by Hadfield and Magelssen (2006). Stain is associated with the wood borer holes, and most sapwood is stained by the end of the second year. Bark beetles and ambrosia beetles show little interest in western larch.

Despite the insect attacks, decay is minimal in western larch. Even in the fifth year after tree death, decay spots are usually small, affecting little volume. With little decay, tree breakage is minimal, and western larch have a low rate of snag failure.

Relations Among Wood Quality Changes and Economic Values

Visual Classification Systems

In many cases, time since death of a tree is unknown. Visual assessments or classification systems have proved useful in the past to address wood quality changes and their effect on product volume and value recovery. Often, visual inspection of a tree may provide clues to the extent of deterioration, although not necessarily to the extent of decay. Parry and colleagues (1996) offered a visual assessment checklist to estimate years since death of beetle-killed trees to aid in sample selection. Snellgrove and Cahill (1980) first applied a visual characteristic classification to the tree before attempting to establish time since death from entomological characteristics. They were unable to accurately estimate mortality date. The following categories have also been used in selecting samples (Lowell and Willits 1998, Snellgrove and Fahey 1977) and differentiating value loss. These classes may be useful in field inspections to classify dying or dead conifers:

Visual assessment of trees is useful in addressing wood quality changes.

Class	Indicators	Significance
Class 1	Live trees or recently attacked trees, still have green needles	Wood quality is likely unchanged
Class 2	Fading or brown-red needles, fine twigs remaining, crown with reddish cast	Often minor changes in wood quality, especially if beetles have introduced stain
Class 3	No fine twigs, tree takes on gray coloration, 90 percent or more of bark remaining	Loss of volume (and value) for solid wood products
Class 4	Less than 90 percent of bark remaining; bark is sloughing off; may be obvious weather checks; gray, weathered coloration	Increased safety issues for both harvesting operators and recreation area users; limited product recovery possible

Figures 12a and 12b show the lumber grade recovery for fire-killed western white pine appearance-grade lumber (Snellgrove and Cahill 1980) and beetle-killed lutz spruce structural lumber (Lowell and Willits 1998), respectively. Although visual classification systems differed slightly, each adequately differentiated product quality and quantity for product type.

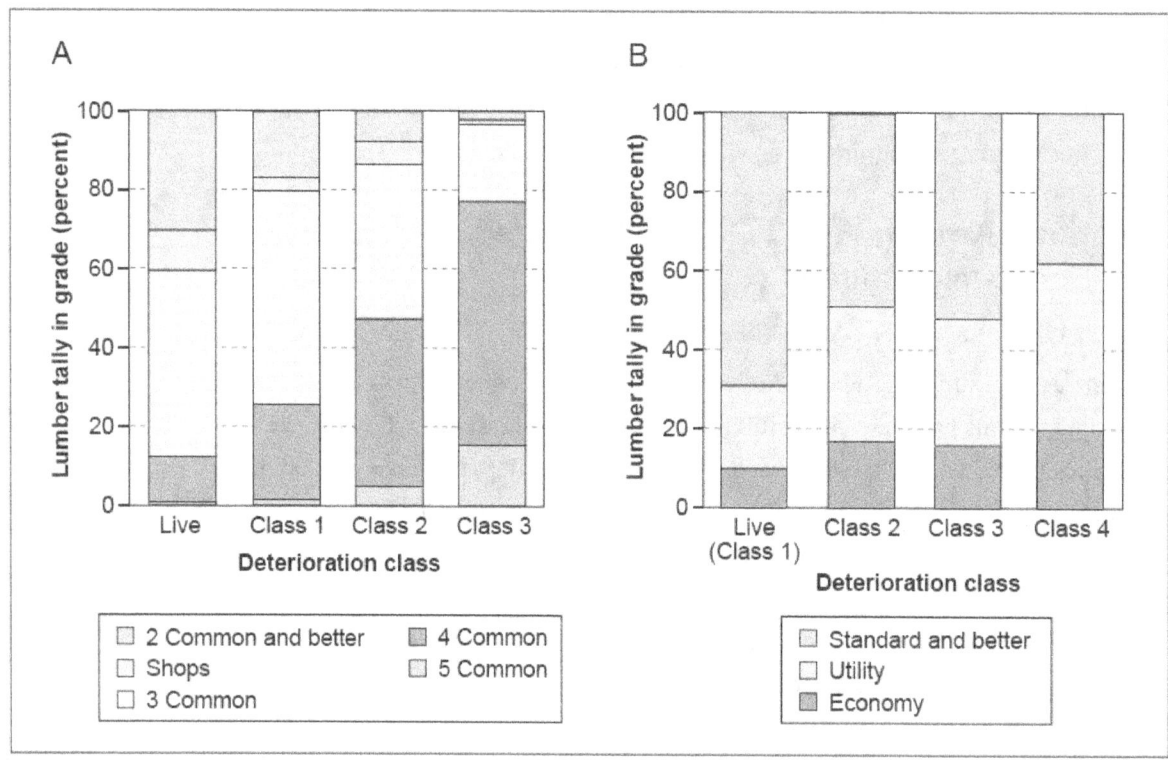

Figure 12—Applicability of visual classification system of defect for (A) fire-killed white pine appearance-grade products (Snellgrove and Cahill 1980) (B) beetle-killed spruce for structural lumber (Lowell and Willits 1998). X-axis deterioration classes differ between studies.

Types of Loss

Volume and value losses are not the same.

There are two types of losses in trees of concern to manufacturers that occur as a result of mortality from disturbance. Volume loss is a function of the extent of deterioration that occurs (e.g., weather checks, decay) decreasing the amount of wood product that can be manufactured from a log or tree. Value loss is a function of the types of product that can be manufactured or their resulting quality (e.g., often measured in terms of lumber grade). Lumber value is lost in two ways: reduction in product volume and a reduction in wood quality. Deterioration effects can result in volume loss, value loss, or both. Deterioration from fire and insect mortality occurs from the exterior of the tree working inward toward the pith. Existing rots (e.g., heart rot or butt rot) should not be considered as contributing to volume losses from disturbance. Forms of deterioration that influence loss include char, stain, decay, breakage, worm holes, and cracking (weather check). Char is the most visible sign of a fire-killed tree, but negligible amounts of useable wood are lost because of it (Hadfield and Magelssen 2006). Stem breakage (Hadfield and Magelssen 2006) also contributes little volume loss the first few years after death.

Product options have a significant impact on economic value of deteriorating wood. Figure 13 displays a range of products in increasing size and quality from the bottom to the top. The effect on solid wood products (e.g., lumber and veneer), which tend to have higher values, is greater than on products manufactured from chips or fibers. In terms of wood quality, the lowest value product would be "dirty chips," suitable for hog fuel or industrial wood pellets. Clean chips (no bark or char) can be used in a variety of products such as pulp and paper or panel products (e.g., particle board, oriented strand board). Char would affect the production of clean chips available for these products. Although not much research has been conducted on oriented strand board (Forintek Canada Corp. 2006) and particle board manufactured from dead materials, several studies have been conducted on pulp and paper manufactured from beetle-killed trees. Processing and properties differences were noted by Werner and colleagues (1983) for white spruce, Thomas (1986) for trees killed by mountain pine beetle, and Scott and colleagues (1996) for beetle-killed lutz spruce. The manufacture of wood-plastic composites using beetle-killed lutz spruce was researched by Yadama and colleagues (2009). Veneer (Wang and

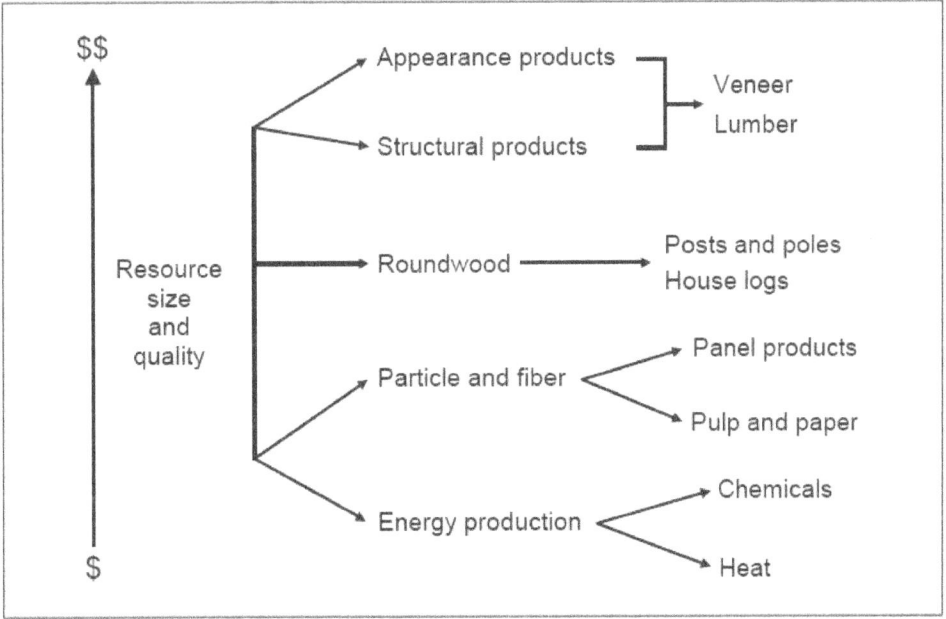

Figure 13—Typical processing streams for wood based on resource size and quality, starting with smaller, lower value at base and increasing in value toward top (vertical axis).

Dai 2008) and plywood (Wang et al. 2008) manufactured from mountain-pine-beetle-killed lodgepole pine were studied in response to the current outbreak of mountain pine beetle. Fahey (1980b) reported on several product opportunities for dead lodgepole pine. Table 7 shows some of his findings on market, demand, and possible usable volume per acre. Even when no manufacturing facilities provide product options, firewood may be an available local market.

Table 7—Product options for dead lodgepole pine

Product	Value/ton	Demand	Volume/acre available	Probable market
	Dollars (1980)		*Percent*	
Power poles	300–400	Small	5–15	Small
House logs	110–260	Moderate	30–60	Moderate
Corral poles	120–150	Small	10–20	Small
Dimension lumber	90–130	Large	70–85	Large
Studs	80–120	Large	70–85	Large
Veneer	90–130	Small	60–75	Moderate
Paper (chips)	35–50	Moderate	90	Variable
Particleboard (furnish)	5–15	None	90	None
Fuel	30–55	Small	95	Possible

Table from Fahey (1980b).

Species play a significant role in product options. Douglas-fir, hemlock, and spruce are typically used in structural lumber products that allow no decay but permit stain. Pine species, historically used for higher value appearance products such as moulding and millwork, do not allow any stain or decay in the highest grades. The presence of stain can reduce the value of a piece of 5/4 No. 1 Shop lumber by more than 50 percent (WWPA 2007).

Volume Loss

Product volume is lost because of checking, decay, breakage, and char. Weather checking, depending on the size of tree and depth of crack, can lower solid wood volume recovery from a log. Decay decreases the volume of wood recoverable. All volume loss translates directly to value loss because of decreased recovery of product.

Assessing volume losses—

Measurement questions abound when assessing dead, dying, and damaged timber. No discussion of volume loss can occur without consideration of the measurement system used to determine the extent of loss. Scalers estimate the amount of defect in a log using different measurement systems including Scribner (USDA FS 1991) and cubic (USDA FS 1985) rules. Snellgrove and Cahill (1980) found that the scaling method used to estimate defect results in differing amounts of defect. Net Scribner and cubic product potential had a tendency to overestimate defect amounts, whereas net cubic scale underestimated defect. Scribner scale, which uses the log small-end diameter as the scaling cylinder, would not make any deductions for deterioration on the large end of the log outside of that scaling cylinder (e.g., sap rot close to the bark). Scribner scale is not very accurate at estimating useable volume in logs from dead trees, in part because it does not take taper into account when estimating log volume (Parry et al. 1996). However, Parry and colleagues (1996) found that defect estimation (by scalers) was unbiased and accurate.

Certain defects also pose problems for measurement specialists. Product recovery studies (Cahill 1980, Snellgrove and Cahill 1980) found Scribner scale overestimated the volume lost from weather checks (cracks). Alternative valuation measurements were proposed by Combes (1978). Insect activity within months following fire led the National Cubic Measurement Committee to request a study on massed worm holes and a proposed new scaling rule. In assessing the applicability of the new rule, Lowell and Parry (2007) recommended that the loss be handled in the valuation (appraisal) process, not the measurement (scaling) process. This is because the damage was not significant enough to justify a volume deduction, although grade loss would result in lower value.

Several studies have shown that there is not much difference in cubic lumber recovery (Lowell and Willits 1998, Parry et al. 1996) and recovery of core-stock veneer (Snellgrove and Ernst 1983) between live and recently dead logs. Differences were found when trees were dead for a longer period. Snellgrove and Fahey (1977) found an average of 8 percent difference in volume recovery between live and up to 2-year-dead true firs. In white pine, they found more differentiation in volume loss across time since death with volume loss gradually decreasing 12 percent from live to over 7 years dead.

When estimating loss, end product and market potential must also be taken into account. Because deterioration from fire and insect activity works inward on the bole, products such as chips that would use the whole log might incur higher volume losses than lumber products, which square off the log so some of the deteriorated wood gets removed as slabs and edgings.

Value Loss

Tree and log grades were developed to provide an initial assessment of quality differences in the resource. Parry and colleagues (1996) found that log grades did not reflect any statistically significant value differences between live and dead Douglas-fir and grand fir. Log scaling, while designed to evaluate volume recovery, does not always reflect value loss. Even though there is little or no difference in scaled defect amount, there can be loss in value from live to dead trees (Snellgrove and Fahey 1977). Product potential, which strongly influences value and is species dependent, can change rapidly after a tree dies. One thing to keep in mind is that lumber prices are constantly changing and not necessarily proportionate to one another. Research results reported here on value loss represent the prices at the time of analysis and may not be reflective of loss that would be incurred at today's prices.

Appearance-grade lumber generally commands a higher value per board foot. High-grade lumber products such as Select, Moulding, and Shop grade lumber, do not allow blue stain. Blue-stained lumber is typically assigned a much lower grade with a significant drop in value, but not necessarily a reduction in volume (Lowell and Parry 2007, Lowell et al. 1992). For example, in ponderosa pine, blue stain causes significant reduction in value after 1 year (Fahey 1980a). Willits and colleagues (1990) found that beetle-killed, small-diameter ponderosa pine in Colorado lost about 10 percent of value in 2 years and 17 percent of value after 3 to 5 years, primarily because of blue stain. Differences in value loss between these two studies can be attributed to the differences in grade cut from the live sample and prices at the time. Snellgrove and Fahey (1977) also found value decreased as time since death increased because of the salvageable lumber drop from higher to lower grades and a decrease in lumber widths produced. Losses in volume of the most valuable products (No. 2 Common and Better and Shops) occurred quickly. Trees dead 1 to 2 years produced 21 percent less volume of lumber in these grades than did live trees. Less and less of these grades were produced the longer trees were dead. Trees dead 3 or more years produced larger volumes of lower value lumber (more than 90 percent 3, 4, and 5 Common). The rapid decline in dollars per thousand board feet lumber tally (DMLT) value they found for white pine is illustrated in the following tabulation:

Years since death	DMLT value
	Percent
Live	100
1 to 2	78
2 to 6	57
7+	45

In structural-grade lumber and veneer, checks, but not stain, reduce the value (Fahey et al. 1986). Depending on the market a sawmill has, end checks may be trimmed, thus trading volume recovery for a corresponding increase in grade. Byrne and colleagues (2005) reported the checks (in logs) and splits (in lumber)

Blue stain in pine lumber causes a significant reduction in value after 1 year.

decreased overall product recovery by reducing board length and width in lodge-pole pine. For Engelmann spruce, Cahill (1980) found a significant reduction in lumber grade between live trees and those dead for more than 20 years, and also attributed the decrease to splits in lumber. Parry and colleagues (1996) found that grand fir did not lose as much value as expected. In contrast, immediate harvest of fire-killed white spruce in interior Alaska was recommended to maintain lumber value (Willits and Sampson 1988).

Volume and Value

When considering both volume and value loss in dead and dying timber, size of tree, years since death, proximity of processing facilities, and current market conditions need to be taken into consideration. If no processing or manufacturing facilities are available, or if they are too far away from the resource, it is probably not economical to remove the dead trees. Figure 14 illustrates how size of log influences what grades may be recovered and where in the log these grades of lumber are produced once the logs get into the mill. Volume recovery may be maximized

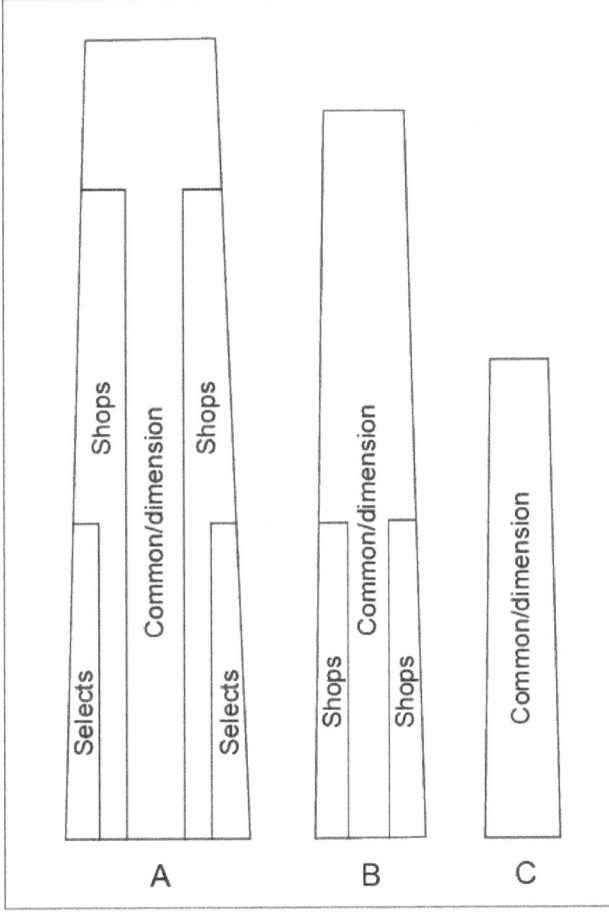

Figure 14—Location in a log where lumber grades are typically produced. Larger logs generally produce higher value lumber such as Selects and Shops (a) than do smaller logs (c). Mid-size logs (b) produce some higher value (Shops) lumber along with the lower value products Common and Dimension lumber (Ayer-Sachet and Fahey 1987). Tree/log size and product affect value lost when processing logs from dead and dying timber.

by salvaging the small, young-growth stands first, but value recovery may be greater by salvaging the mature stands first (Aho and Cahill 1984).

Losses in value and volume depend on species, product produced, and time since death. Current markets for byproducts (e.g., chips) and their proximity to primary processing facilities also influence value loss. Case studies on wood products manufactured from dead and dying trees are presented in figures 15, 16, and 17. Figure 15 illustrates volume, lumber grade, and value recovery differences in ponderosa pine appearance-grade products. Results from a Douglas-fir and grand fir study (Parry et al. 1996) are shown in figure 16. The graphs of lumber tally from dead logs show how wood quality differences affect lumber grade recovery for each species. Figure 17 shows the complexity of estimating volume lost from dead trees. The variability in volume recovery for lodgepole pine is based on resource characteristics (size and time since death) and product options. It also illustrates that time since death does not always significantly affect volume recovery. Fahey and colleagues (1986) did find significant value loss differences among mills, and the amount of value loss was strongly related to the availability of a chip market. They also noted that there were greater value losses in the board mill, and that stud mills lost the least value.

Another potential loss to volume and value is the loss during logging and manufacturing of dead timber. First, losses in volume and value can result from increased breakage during logging and handling as time since death increases (Snellgrove and Fahey 1977). Extra handling to reduce potential breakage adds to the logging costs, reducing financial returns to landowners. Second, logs from dead trees have reduced moisture content, which can increase manufacturing costs, reducing financial returns to processors. There are also potential costs associated with mitigating the effect of dirt and rocks in the cracks of dead timber on processing equipment.

Appendix 2 contains a list of studies by species that address differences in volume and value recovery between live and dead trees. It is difficult to synthesize data from these studies, as they were conducted at different mills, the product mix differed, and resource characteristics were not the same. However, the studies listed in appendix 2 provide reference results useful in assessing volume and value recovery.

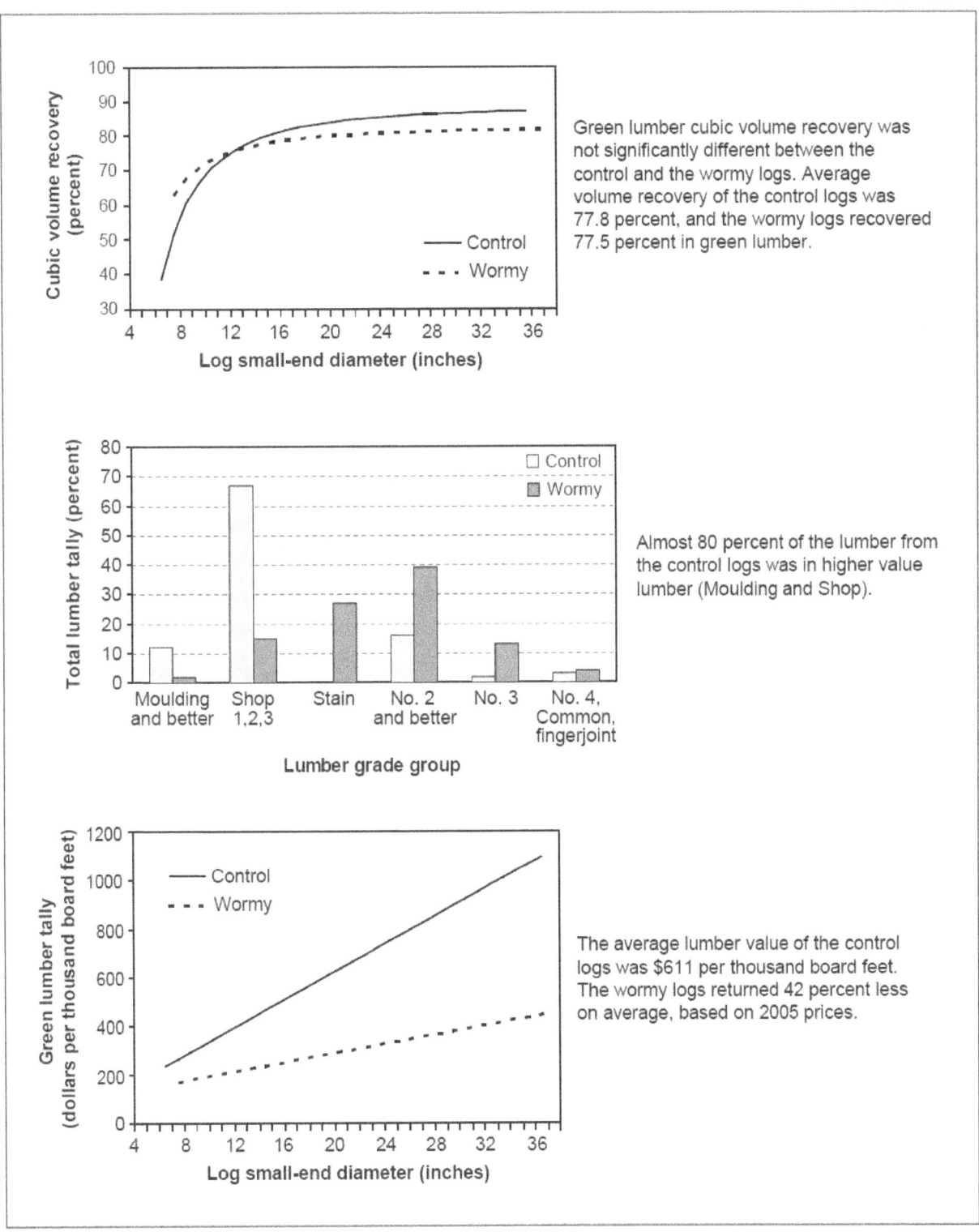

Figure 15—Case study 1. This case study illustrates that volume and value recovery are not the same to a manufacturer. This is especially true in appearance-grade products. These results are for fire-killed, 1-year-dead ponderosa pine from southern Oregon (Lowell and Parry 2007).

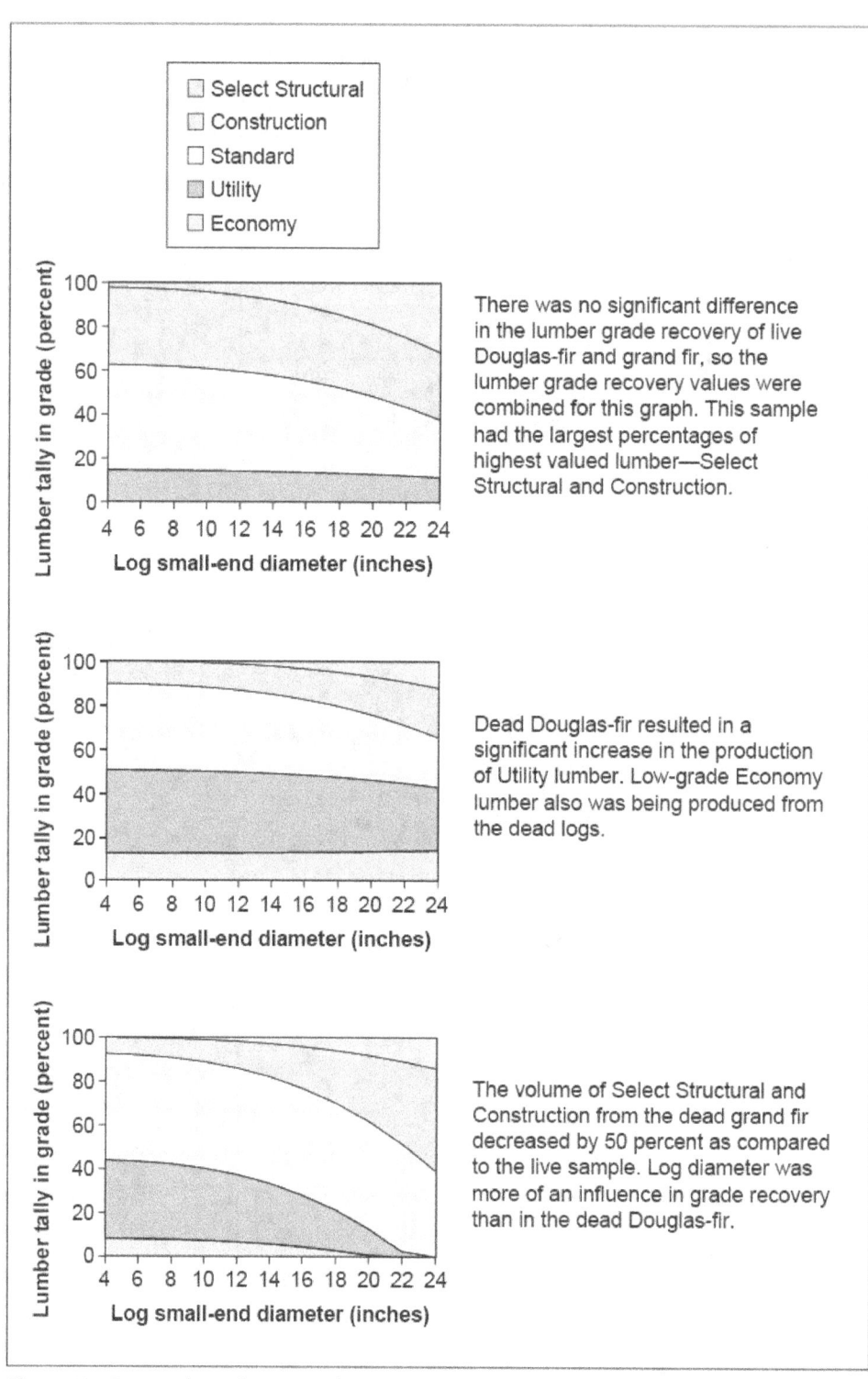

Figure 16—Case study 2. The case study presented here demonstrated that species has a role in deterioration rate and product recovery as shown with results from a study on beetle-killed Douglas-fir and grand fir in eastern Oregon. The grand fir did not deteriorate as fast as the Douglas-fir or lose as much value as expected (Parry et al. 1996).

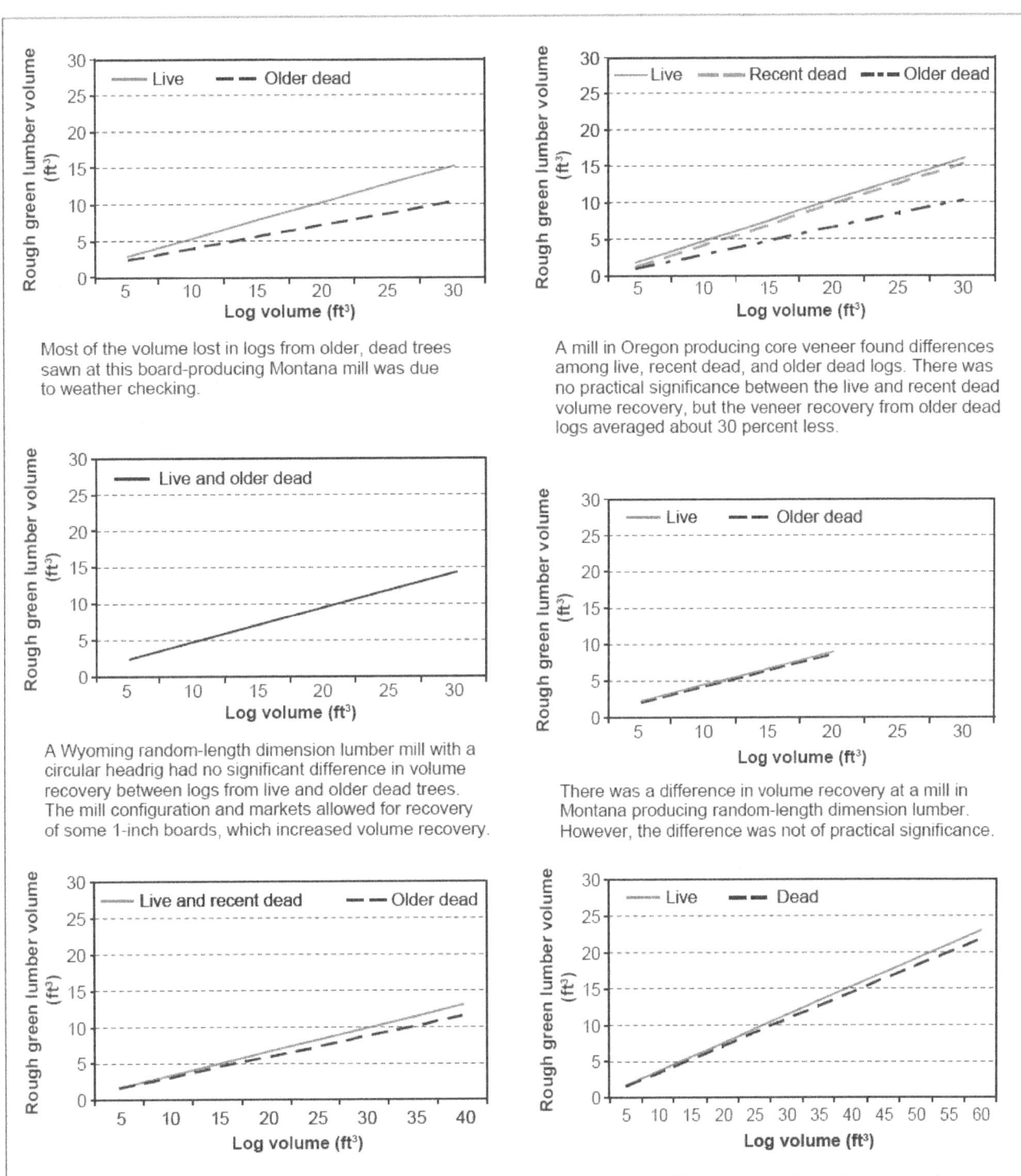

Most of the volume lost in logs from older, dead trees sawn at this board-producing Montana mill was due to weather checking.

A mill in Oregon producing core veneer found differences among live, recent dead, and older dead logs. There was no practical significance between the live and recent dead volume recovery, but the veneer recovery from older dead logs averaged about 30 percent less.

A Wyoming random-length dimension lumber mill with a circular headrig had no significant difference in volume recovery between logs from live and older dead trees. The mill configuration and markets allowed for recovery of some 1-inch boards, which increased volume recovery.

There was a difference in volume recovery at a mill in Montana producing random-length dimension lumber. However, the difference was not of practical significance.

No difference in volume recovery was found between logs from live and recent-dead trees sawn at an Oregon stud mill. The older dead did have significantly lower recovery.

Time since death was not a factor for logs sawn at a Wyoming stud mill. The live sample did have a significantly greater volume recovery than the dead classes combined.

Figure 17—Case study 3. The influence of mill, geographic location, and product are shown for beetle-killed lodgepole pine (adapted from Fahey et al. 1986). Each graph shows the relationship of gross cubic feet of log volume to cubic feet of rough green lumber from live trees and trees at different times since death (recent and older dead).

Conclusions

There are many factors to take into consideration when determining what action to take following a natural disturbance. Managers must weigh the pros and cons of leaving or removing dead or dying trees in a stand. There are no right answers and tradeoffs are many. Alternatives exist, each with their own set of consequences, and many are highly time specific.

Leaving dead trees can provide habitat for forest organisms (birds, mammals, insects, fungi—some rare or endangered, some decomposers) although these organisms may be different from those that were there predisturbance. As trees decompose, nutrient cycling occurs. Erosion is reduced by not harvesting the timber. However, dead and dying trees may also harbor organisms that can spread to and infect adjacent live stands. Loss of recreation opportunities can occur, as standing dead trees are often considered safety hazards especially near or in campgrounds or other recreation sites. Natural disturbances (e.g., stand-replacement fire) can lead to densely stocked stands where successional patterns involve heavy natural regeneration. These stands are further susceptible to increased mortality from insect and disease epidemics adding to dry fuel loads.

There are equally compelling arguments for removing dead and dying trees. One of the foremost is the need to manage the increased risk of wildfires, especially severe wildfires with their increased cost of fire suppression, possible loss of lives, destruction of property, and the attendant alteration of other ecosystem services such as wildlife habitat, water quality, viewsheds, recreation opportunities, and carbon sequestration. There are also financial issues when dead and dying trees represent potential financial gains and losses to timberland owners. In these cases, rapid action is required to minimize capital losses to timberland owners.

Both the size of trees involved and time since disturbance influence available management options. First, tree size, as shown in tables 2 through 6, influences rates of decay and breakage. Generally small trees (say less than 10 in d.b.h.) will be difficult to remove in economically feasible operations. This will make activities to reduce hazardous fuels in the wildland-urban interface expensive when they involve small-diameter stands that have either been damaged or have the potential for damage by disturbance agents.

Second, increased time since disturbance alters some of the outcomes. Blue stain in pines significantly reduces the value recovery of pines generally within 1 year postfire. Two to four years after tree death, it is still possible to recover some wood products, but with losses in both value and volume. Understory vegetation that has started to reestablish itself will be disturbed. There is potential for loss of some forest organisms while perhaps creating habitat for other species. Soil disturbance could be mitigated through choice of harvesting technology.

Waiting more than 4 years following disturbance to harvest a stand limits product options. It may be desirable to use some of the wood from the dead trees, but harvesting and transportation costs in conjunction with available wood products markets need to be considered. Product options change as markets change. Prestemon and colleagues (2006) found that salvage harvests can play an important role in mitigating the timber-related economic impacts of fire. They also found that the effects of delaying salvage following a catastrophic wildfire can be substantial, increasing losses or reducing potential gains by millions of dollars. For timber-based communities, availability of wood to keep manufacturing facilities operating is important. The deteriorating quality of wood over time may make it uneconomical to harvest, transport, and process.

There are long-term consequences for the forest depending on the size and severity of fire and other disturbances. Regenerating and damaged stands may look very different from what was there originally. These changes in stand attributes and structure may change the human-forest interactions leading to changes in management goals. Given desired future stand conditions, harvesting dead and dying trees, planting seedlings, and performing active management may be required to restore lost functions. Postfire regeneration of stands can alter vegetative composition and impact the role that forests play in climate change. Such efforts can help offset the loss of carbon stored in trees that was consumed when burned (contributing to atmospheric carbon). In the context of carbon sequestration, these losses, the carbon stored in dead trees, and the carbon stored in wood products that might be manufactured from salvaged logs are all part of changes in the carbon balance.

Options involving active forest management have been complicated by the relentless changes in forest products markets and the processing sector (see Haynes 2008 for a discussion). The number of forest products manufacturing facilities has decreased (although the size of lumber manufacturing mills has increased) over the last two decades. The ongoing (2008–2009) economic difficulties coupled with additional losses of timber resources may lead to closure of more mills and the loss of employment associated with them. This loss of industry infrastructure complicates active forest management, especially that undertaken to reduce hazardous fuel in the wildland-urban interface. It also complicates sustainable development opportunities for communities adjacent to forests.

The information and data we present provide tools for land managers. Such tools can help land managers to make informed decisions on how to proceed following a disturbance. Such decisions will shape future forests and influence the flow of goods and services.

Glossary

cambium—Layer of living cells between the innermost bark of a tree (phloem) and the wood (xylem) (Helms 1998).

conk—Visible sporophore or fruiting body of a wood-destroying fungus living inside a tree or log (Helms 1998).

decay—Decomposition of wood by fungi and bacteria; softens and weakens wood. Visual clues include changes in texture and color of wood (Helms 1998).

deterioration—Changes that make wood unsuitable for use. "Decay" refers specifically to fungal or bacterial decay. "Deterioration" refers to damage from insects, fire, or weather. "Limited deterioration" describes changes such as blue stain that affect the character of wood and thus reduce the value, but do not weaken the wood or reduce the volume of wood (Kimmey and Furniss 1943).

diameter at breast height (d.b.h.)—Diameter of tree bole measured at breast height (4.5 ft or 1.37 m from the ground) (Helms 1998).

frass—Wood dust and waste product produced from insect feeding on trees (Helms 1998).

heartwood—Inner, nonliving wood of the tree bole; generally identifiable as darker colored wood, in contrast to lighter colored sapwood (Helms 1998).

hyphae—The filaments of a mycelium (Helms 1998).

mycelium (plural, mycelia)—The vegetative part of a fungus (Helms 1998). Composed of threadlike filaments that take various forms (Allaby 2005), depending on species; may look like network of fine threads or may form mats, plaques, or paperlike layers in wood.

phloem—Layer just inside the tree bark; phloem transports food from the leaves to the bole and roots (Helms 1998).

sapwood—The outer layers of the tree bole; generally identifiable as lighter colored wood, in contrast to darker colored heartwood (Helms 1998).

Scribner scale [Note: Society of American Foresters gives this term as "Scribner rule."]—A diagram log rule that assumes 1-in (2.54-cm) boards and 0.25-in (0.64-cm) kerf, is based on diameter at the small end of the log, disregards taper, and does not provide for overrun; … underestimates lumber yield on small logs and on long logs with taper (Helms 1998).

small diameter/large diameter—In this report, "small-diameter" refers to trees under 10 inches d.b.h., and "large-diameter" refers to trees over 15 inches d.b.h.

sporophore—A reproductive structure in fungi that produces spores (Helms 1998).

stain—Wood color changes caused by fungi. Discoloration of wood caused by fungi; generally blue, green, or black (Helms 1998).

volume—The most accurate way of measuring product volume recovered from a log is cubic recovery (CR) percentage because it uses cubic volume for both lumber and log (Parry et al. 1996).

value—The most accurate measure of inherent wood value is dollars per thousand board feet lumber tally (DMLT) because it is based only on the lumber actually produced from a log and does not entail any estimated deductions for defects (Parry et al. 1996).

Acknowledgments

This synthesis is funded in part by the National Fire Plan and responds to needs identified in portfolios C and D. The authors acknowledge Andris Eglitis and Peter Powers for their extensive review of this manuscript and their regional insights.

Metric Equivalents

When you know:	Multiply by:	To find:
Inches (in)	2.54	Centimeters
Feet (ft)	.305	Meters
Cubic feet (ft^3)	.0283	Cubic meters
Degrees Fahrenheit	.55(°F - 32)	Degrees Celsius

Literature Cited

Aho, P.E.; Cahill, J.M. 1984. Deterioration rates of blowdown timber and potential problems associated with product recovery. Gen. Tech. Rep. PNW-GTR-167. Portland, OR: U.S. Department of Agriculture, Forest Service, Pacific Northwest Research Station. 11 p.

Allaby, M. 2005. Oxford dictionary of ecology. New York, NY: Oxford University Press. 473 p.

Ayer-Sachet, J.K.; Fahey, T.D. 1987. Lumber volume and value from ponderosa pine. In: Baumgartner, D.M.; Lotan, J.E., eds. Ponderosa pine: the species and its management. Symposium proceedings. Pullman, WA: Washington State University Cooperative Extension Service: 11–17.

Beal, J.A.; Kimmey, J.W.; Rapraeger, E.F. 1935. Deterioration of fire-killed Douglas-fir. The Timberman. 37(2): 12–17.

Bevins, C.D. 1980. Estimating survival and salvage potential of fire-scarred Douglas-fir. Res. Pap. INT-287. Ogden, UT: U.S. Department of Agriculture, Forest Service, Intermountain Forest and Range Experiment Station. 8 p.

Black, S.H. 2005. Logging to control insects: the science and myths behind managing forest insect "pests." A synthesis of independently reviewed research. Portland, OR: The Xerces Society for Invertebrate Conservation. 82 p.

Boyce, J.S. 1929. Deterioration of wind-thrown timber on the Olympic Peninsula, Washington. Tech. Bull. 104. Washington, DC: U.S. Department of Agriculture. 28 p.

Brown, J.K.; Reinhardt, E.D.; Kramer, K.A. 2003. Coarse woody debris: managing benefits and fire hazard in the recovering forest. Gen. Tech. Rep. RMRS-GTR-105. Ogden, UT: U.S. Department of Agriculture, Forest Service, Rocky Mountain Research Station. 16 p.

Brown, J.K.; Smith, J.K. 2000. Wildland fire in ecosystems: effects of fire on flora. Gen. Tech. Rep. RMRS-GTR-42. Ogden, UT: U.S. Department of Agriculture, Forest Service, Rocky Mountain Research Station. 257 p. Vol. 2

Byrne, A.; Stonestreet, C.; Peter, B. 2005. Current knowledge of characteristics and utilization of post-mountain pine beetle wood in solid wood products. Mountain pine beetle initiative working paper 2005-8. Vancouver, BC: Forintek Canada Corporation. 18 p.

Cahill, J.M. 1980. Preliminary lumber recovery for dead and live Engelmann spruce. Res. Note PNW-365. Portland, OR: U.S. Department of Agriculture, Forest Service, Pacific Northwest Forest and Range Experiment Station. 11 p.

Carpenter, S.E.; Harmon, M.E.; Ingham, E.R.; Kelsey, R.G.; Lattin, J.D.; Schowalter, T.D. 1988. Early patterns of heterotroph activity in conifer logs. In: Boddy, L.; Watling, R.; Lyon, A., eds. Fungi and ecological disturbance. Proceedings of the Royal Society of Edinburgh. 94(B): 33–43.

Cartwright, K.St.G.; Findlay, W.P.K. 1958. Decay of timber and its prevention. 2nd ed. London, United Kingdom: Her Majesty's Stationery Office. 332 p.

Combes, J.A. 1978. Valuation alternatives for dead timber. In: Symposium: the dead softwood timber resource. Pullman, WA. Engineering Extension Service Washington State University: 169–176.

Connaughton, C.A. 1936. Fire damage in the ponderosa pine type in Idaho. Journal of Forestry. 34(1): 46–51.

DeNitto, G.; Cramer, B.; Gibson, K.; Lockman, B.; McConnell, T.; Stipe, L.; Sturdevant, N.; Taylor, J. 2000. Survivability and deterioration of fire-injured trees in the northern Rocky Mountains: a review of the literature. Forest Health Protection Report 2000-13. Missoula, MT: U.S. Department of Agriculture, Forest Service, Northern Region. 27 p.

Dieterich, J.H. 1979. Recovery potential of the fire-damaged southwestern ponderosa pine. Res. Note RN-379. Fort Collins, CO: U.S. Department of Agriculture, Forest Service, Rocky Mountain Forest and Range Experiment Station. 8 p.

Edmonds, R.L.; Eglitis, A. 1989. The role of the Douglas-fir beetle and wood borers in the decomposition of and nutrient release from Douglas-fir logs. Canadian Journal of Forestry Research. 19: 853–859.

Everett, R.; Lehmkuhl, J.; Schellhaas, R.; Ohlson, P.; Keenum, D.; Riesterer, H.; Spurbeck, D. 1999. Snag dynamics in a chronosequence of 26 wildfires on the east slope of the Cascade Range in Washington State, USA. International Journal of Wildland Fire. 9(4): 223–234.

Fahey, T.D. 1980a. Beetle-killed pine can be salvaged, but for how long? Forest Industries. 107(5): 60–61.

Fahey, T.D. 1980b. Evaluating dead lodgepole pine for products. Forest Products Journal. 30(12): 34–39.

Fahey, T.D.; Sachet, J.; Willits, S. 1990. Evaluation of fire-killed ponderosa pine for volume and value loss. 7 p. Unpublished report. On file with: Eini Lowell, U.S. Department of Agriculture, Forest Service, Pacific Northwest Research Station, 620 SW Main St., Suite 400, Portland, OR 97205.

Fahey, T.D.; Snellgrove, T.A.; Plank, M.E. 1986. Changes in product recovery between live and dead lodgepole pine: a compendium. Res. Pap. PNW-RP-353. Portland, OR: U.S. Department of Agriculture, Forest Service, Pacific Northwest Research Station. 25 p.

Farr, D.F.; Bills, G.F.; Chamuris, G.P.; Rossman, A.Y. 1989. Fungi on plants and plant products in the United States. St. Paul, MN: American Phytopathological Society Press. 1252 p.

Flint, C.G.; McFarlane, B.; Müller, M. 2008. Human dimensions of forest disturbance by insects: an international synthesis. Environmental Management. 43(6): 1174-1186. DOI: 10.1007/s00267-008-9193-4.

Forintek Canada Corp. 2006. Rehydrated beetle-killed wood has potential as oriented strandboard feedstock. Specialty Wood Journal. 9(2): 6, 8.

Fowler, J.F.; Sieg, C.H. 2004. Postfire mortality of ponderosa pine and Douglas-fir: a review of methods to predict tree death. Gen. Tech. Rep. RMRS-GTR-132. Fort Collins, CO: U.S. Department of Agriculture, Forest Service, Rocky Mountain Research Station. 25 p.

Furniss, R.L. 1937. Salvage on Tillamook Burn as affected by insect activity. The Timberman. 1937(December): 11–13, 30–32.

Furniss, R.L.; Carolin, V.M. 1977. Western forest insects. Misc. Publ. 1339. Washington, DC: U.S. Department of Agriculture. 568 p.

Gibson, K.; Negrón, J.F. 2009. Fire and bark beetle interactions. In: Hayes, J.L.; Lundquist, J.E., comps. Proceedings, The Western Bark Beetle Research Group: a unique collaboration with Forest Health Protection. Gen. Tech. Rep. PNW-GTR-784. Portland, OR: U.S. Department of Agriculture, Forest Service, Pacific Northwest Research Station: 51–69.

Goheen, E.M.; Willhite, E.A. 2006. Field guide to the common diseases and insect pests of Oregon and Washington conifers. R6-NR-FID-PR-01-06. Portland, OR: U.S. Department of Agriculture, Forest Service, Pacific Northwest Region. 327 p.

Hadfield, J.; Magelssen, R. 2006. Wood changes in fire-killed tree species in eastern Washington. Wenatchee, WA: U.S. Department of Agriculture, Forest Service, Okanogan and Wenatchee National Forests. 49 p.

Harrington, T.C.; Furniss, M.M.; Shaw, C.G. 1981. Dissemination of hymenomycetes by *Dendroctonus pseudotsugae* (Coleoptera: Scolytidae). Phytopathology. 71: 551–554.

Harvey, R.D., Jr. 1979. Rate of increase of blue stained volume in mountain pine beetle killed lodgepole pine in northeastern Oregon. Canadian Journal of Forest Research. 9(3): 323–326.

Hayashi, N.; Honda, K.; Hara, S.; Idzumihara, H.; Mikata, K.; Komae, H. 1996. The chemical relationship between fungus and beetles on ponderosa pine. Zeitschrift fur Naturforschung Section C, Biosciences. 51(11–12): 813–817.

Haynes, R.W. 2008. Emergent lessons from a century of experience with Pacific Northwest timber markets. Gen. Tech. Rep. PNW-GTR-747. Portland, OR: U.S. Department of Agriculture, Forest Service, Pacific Northwest Research Station. 45 p.

Helms, J.A., ed. 1998. The dictionary of forestry. Bethesda, MD: The Society of American Foresters. 210 p.

Hood, S.; Bentz, B. 2007. Predicting post-fire Douglas-fir beetle attacks and tree mortality in the Northern Rocky Mountains. Canadian Journal of Forest Research. 37: 1058–1069.

Hood, S.; Bentz, B.; Gibson, K.; Ryan, K.; DeNitto,G. 2007. Assessing post-fire Douglas-fir mortality and Douglas-fir beetle attacks in the northern Rocky Mountains. Gen. Tech. Rep. RMRS-GTR-199. Fort Collins, CO: U.S. Department of Agriculture, Forest Service, Rocky Mountain Research Station. 31 p.

Jackson, M.; Bulaon, B. 2005. Changes in fire-killed western larch on the Glacier View Ranger District (Flathead National Forest, Montana). Years two, three, and four report. Forest Health Protection Report 05-06. Missoula, MT: U.S. Department of Agriculture, Forest Service, Northern Region. 20 p.

Kennedy, R.W. 1958. Strength retention in wood decayed to small weight losses. Forest Products Journal. 8(10): 308–314.

Kimmey, J.W. 1955. Rate of deterioration of fire-killed timber in California. Circular 962. Washington, DC: U.S. Department of Agriculture. 22 p.

Kimmey, J.W.; Furniss, R.L. 1943. Deterioration of fire-killed Douglas-fir. Tech. Bull. 851. Washington, DC: U.S. Department of Agriculture. 61 p.

Lewis, K.J.; Hartley, I. 2005. Rate of deterioration, degrade and fall of trees killed by mountain pine beetle: a synthesis of the literature and experiential knowledge. Mountain Pine Beetle Initiative Working Paper 2005-14. Victoria, BC: Canadian Forest Service. 27 p.

Lindenmayer, D.B.; Noss, R.F. 2006. Salvage logging, ecosystem processes, and biodiversity conservation. Conservation Biology. 20(4): 949–958.

Littke, W.R.; Gara, R.I. 1986. Decay of fire-damaged lodgepole pine in south-central Oregon. Forest Ecology and Management. 17: 279–287.

Lowell, E.C. 2001. Veneer recovery from beetle-killed spruce trees, Kenai Peninsula, Alaska. Western Journal of Applied Forestry. 16(2): 65–70.

Lowell, E.C.; Cahill, J.M. 1996. Deterioration of fire-killed timber in southern Oregon and northern California. Western Journal of Applied Forestry. 11(4): 125–131.

Lowell, E.C.; Parry, D.L. 2007. Value loss in ponderosa pine logs from beetle activity following fire in southern Oregon. Forest Products Journal. 57(7/8): 68–72.

Lowell, E.C.; Willits, S.A. 1998. Lumber recovery from beetle-killed spruce trees on the Kenai Peninsula, Alaska. Western Journal of Applied Forestry. 13(2): 54–59.

Lowell, E.C.; Willits, S.A.; Krahmer, R.L. 1992. Deterioration of fire-killed and fire-damaged timber in the Western United States. Gen. Tech. Rep. PNW-GTR-292. Portland, OR: U.S. Department of Agriculture, Forest Service, Pacific Northwest Research Station. 27 p.

Lundquist, J.E.; Bentz, B.J. 2009. Bark beetles in a changing climate. In: Hayes, J.L.; Lundquist, J.E., comps. Proceedings, The Western Bark Beetle Research Group: a unique collaboration with Forest Health Protection. Gen. Tech. Rep. PNW-GTR-784. Portland, OR: U.S. Department of Agriculture, Forest Service, Pacific Northwest Research Station: 39–49.

Marcot, B.G.; Gunderson, G.; Mellen, K.; Ohmann, J.L. 2004. DecAID advisor, a tool for managing snags, down wood and wood decay in PNW forests. Western Forester. 2004(July/August): 12–13.

Mazza, R. 2007. Managing forests after fire. Science Update 15. Portland, OR: U.S. Department of Agriculture, Forest Service, Pacific Northwest Research Station. 12 p.

McCullough, D.G.; Werner, R.A.; Neumann, D. 1998. Fire and insects in northern and boreal forest ecosystems of North America. Annual Review of Entomology. 43: 107–127.

McHugh, C.W.; Kolb, T.E.; Wilson, J.L. 2003. Bark beetle attacks on ponderosa pine following fire in northern Arizona. Environmental Entomology. 32(3): 510–522.

Mellen, K.; Marcot, B.G.; Ohmann, J.L.; Waddell, K.; Willhite, E.A.; Hostetler, B.B.; Livingston, S.A.; Ogden. C. 2009. DecAID, the decayed wood advisor for managing snags, partially dead trees, and down wood for biodiversity in forests of Washington and Oregon. Version 2.1. Portland, OR: U.S. Department of Agriculture, Forest Service, Pacific Northwest Region and Pacific Northwest Research Station; USDI Fish and Wildlife Service, Oregon State Office. http://www.fs.fed.us/r6/nr/wildlife/decaid/index.shtml. (20 December 2007).

Mitchell, R.G.; Preistler, H.K. 1998. Fall rate of lodgepole pine killed by mountain pine beetle in central Oregon. Western Journal of Applied Forestry. 13(1): 23–26.

Neary, D.G.; Ryan, K.C.; DeBano, L.F. 2005. Wildland fire in ecosystems: effects of fire on soils and water. Gen. Tech. Rep. RMRS-GTR-42. Ogden, UT: U.S. Department of Agriculture, Forest Service, Rocky Mountain Research Station. 250 p. Vol. 4.

Olsen, C.S.; Shindler, B.A. 2007. Citizen-agency interactions in planning and decisionmaking after large wildfires. Gen. Tech. Rep. PNW-GTR-715. Portland, OR: U.S. Department of Agriculture, Forest Service, Pacific Northwest Research Station. 37 p.

Panshin, A.J.; deZeeuw, C. 1964. Wood deterioration and stains; natural durability of wood. In: Textbook of wood technology: volume I. New York: McGraw-Hill Book Co.: 382–389. Chapter 10.

Parker, T.J.; Clancy, K.M.; Mathiasen, R.L. 2006. Interactions among fire, insects and pathogens in coniferous forests of the interior Western United States and Canada. Agricultural and Forest Entomology. 8: 167–189.

Parmeter, J.R., Jr.; Slaughter, G.W.; Chen, M.; Wood, D.L. 1992. Rate and depth of sapwood occlusion following inoculation of pines with bluestain fungi. Forest Science. 38(1): 34–44.

Parry, D.L.; Filip, G.M.; Willits, S.A.; Parks, C.G. 1996. Lumber recovery and deterioration of beetle-killed Douglas-fir and grand fir in the Blue Mountains of eastern Oregon. Gen. Tech. Rep. PNW-GTR-376. Portland, OR: U.S. Department of Agriculture, Forest Service, Pacific Northwest Research Station. 24 p.

Peterson, D.L. 1983. Estimating postfire timber damage with a simulation model. In: Proceedings of the 7th conference on fire and forest meteorology. Boston, MA: American Meteorological Society: 159–162.

Peterson, D.L. 1985. Crown scorch volume and scorch height: estimates of postfire tree condition. Canadian Journal of Forest Research. 15(3): 596–598.

Peterson, D.L.; Agee, J.K.; Aplet, G.H.; Dykstra, D.; Graham, R.T.; Lehmkuhl, J.F.; Pilliod, D.S.; Potts, D.F.; Powers, R.F.; Stuart, J.D. 2009. Effects of timber harvest following wildfire in western North America. Gen. Tech. Rep. PNW-GTR-776. Portland, OR: U.S. Department of Agriculture, Forest Service, Pacific Northwest Research Station. 51 p.

Peterson, D.L.; Evers, L.; Gravenmier, R.A.; Eberhardt, E. 2007. A consumer guide: tools to manage vegetation and fuels. Gen. Tech. Rep. PNW-GTR-690. Portland, OR: U.S. Department of Agriculture, Forest Service, Pacific Northwest Research Station. 151 p.

Prestemon, J.P.; Wear, D.N.; Stewart, F.J.; Holmes, T.P. 2006. Wildfire, timber salvage, and the economics of expediency. Forest Policy and Economics. 8(3): 312–322.

Reeves, G.H.; Bisson, P.A.; Rieman, B.E.; Benda, L.E. 2006. Postfire logging in riparian areas. Conservation Biology. 20(4): 994–1004.

Richmond, H.A.; Lejeune, R.R. 1945. The deterioration of fire-killed white spruce by wood boring insects in northern Saskatchewan. Forestry Chronicles. 21: 168–192.

Ryan, K.C.; Amman, G.D. 1994. Interactions between fire-injured trees and insects in the Greater Yellowstone Area. In: Despain, D.G., ed. Proceedings of Plants and their environments: first biennial scientific conference on the Greater Yellowstone Ecosystem. Tech. Rep. NPS/NRYELL/NRTR. Yellowstone National Park, WY: 259–271.

Ryan, K.C.; Reinhardt, E.D. 1988. Predicting postfire mortality of seven western conifers. Canadian Journal of Forest Research. 18: 1291–1297.

Saab, V.; Block, W.; Russell, R.; Lehmkuhl, J.; Bate, L.; White, R. 2007. Birds and burns of the interior West: descriptions, habitats, and management in western forests. Gen. Tech. Rep. PNW-GTR-712. Portland, OR: U.S. Department of Agriculture, Forest Service, Pacific Northwest Research Station. 23 p.

Sandberg, D.V.; Ottmar, R.D.; Peterson, J.L.; Core, J. 2002. Wildland fire in ecosystems: effects of fire on air. Gen. Tech. Rep. RMRS-GTR-42. Ogden, UT: U.S. Department of Agriculture, Forest Service, Rocky Mountain Research Station. 79 p. Vol. 5

Scott, G.M.; Bormett, D.W.; Sutherland, N.R.; Abubakr, S.; Lowell, E. 1996. Pulpability of beetle-killed spruce. Res. Pap. FPL-RP-557. Madison, WI: U.S. Department of Agriculture, Forest Service, Forest Products Laboratory. 8 p.

Sieg, C.H.; McMillin, J.D.; Fowler, J.F.; Allen, K.K.; Negron, J.F.; Wadleigh, L.L.; Anhold, J.A.; Gibson, K.E. 2006. Best predictors for postfire mortality of ponderosa pine trees in the intermountain West. Forest Science. 52(6): 718–728.

Smith, J.K., ed. 2000. Wildland fire in ecosystems: effects of fire on fauna. Gen. Tech. Rep. RMRS-GTR-42. Ogden, UT: U.S. Department of Agriculture, Forest Service, Rocky Mountain Research Station. 83 p. Vol. 1.

Smith, R.B.; Craig, H.M.; Chu, D. 1970. Fungal deterioration of second growth Douglas-fir logs in coastal British Columbia. Canadian Journal of Botany. 48(9): 1541–1551.

Smith, R.B.; Graham, R.D.; Morrell, J.J. 1987. Influence of air-seasoning on fungal colonization and strength properties of Douglas-fir pole sections. Forest Products Journal. 37(9): 45–48.

Snellgrove, T.A.; Cahill, J.M. 1980. Dead western white pine: characteristics, product recovery, and problems associated with utilization. Res. Pap. PNW-270. Portland, OR: U.S. Department of Agriculture, Forest Service, Pacific Northwest Forest and Range Experiment Station. 63 p.

Snellgrove, T.A.; Ernst, S. 1983. Veneer recovery from live and dead lodgepole pine. Forest Products Journal. 33(6): 21–26.

Snellgrove, T.A.; Fahey, T.D. 1977. Market values and problems associated with utilization of dead timber. Forest Products Journal. 27(10): 74–79.

Thies, W.G.; Niwa, C.G.; Westlind, D.J. 2001. Impact of prescribed fires in ponderosa pine stands in the southern Blue Mountains on various components of the ecosystem–three years post fire. In: Marshall, K., ed. Proceedings of the forty-ninth western international forest disease work conference. Central Point, OR: Southwest Oregon Forest Insect and Disease Service Center: 25–30.

Thies, W.G.; Westlind, D.J.; Loewen, M.; Brenner, G. 2006. Prediction of delayed mortality of fire-damaged ponderosa pine following prescribed fires in eastern Oregon, USA. International Journal of Wildand Fire. 15(1): 19–29.

Thomas, G.P.; Craig, H.M. 1958. Deterioration by fungi of killed Douglas-fir in interior British Columbia. Ottawa, ON: Forest Biology Division, Canada Department of Agriculture. 20 p.

Thomas, P.R. 1986 Infestation of pine and spruce bark beetles in British Columbia and its effect on kraft and mechanical pulping. In: Nielson, R.W., ed. Proceedings of harvesting and processing of beetle-killed timber. Vancouver, BC: Forintek Canada Corp., Western Division.

Thompson, J.R.; Spies, T.A.; Ganio, L.M. 2007. Reburn severity in managed and unmanaged vegetation in a large wildfire. Proceedings of the National Academy of Sciences. 104(25): 10743–10748.

U.S. Department of Agriculture, Forest Service [USDA FS]. 1985. National forest log scaling handbook. FSH 2409.11 Amend. 6. Washington, DC.

U.S. Department of Agriculture, Forest Service [USDA FS]. 1991. National forest cubic scaling handbook. FSH 2409.11a. Amend. 2409.11a-91-1. Washington, DC.

U.S. Department of Agriculture, Forest Service [USDA FS]. 2005. Pacific Northwest forest inventory and analysis. Statewide inventory results. http://www.fs.fed.us/pnw/fia/statewide_results/index.shtml. (20 December 2007).

U.S. Department of Agriculture, Forest Service [USDA FS]. 2006. Interior West forest inventory and analysis. Inventory results. http://www.fs.fed.us/rm/ogden/publications/index.shtml. (20 December 2007).

van Mantgem, P.J.; Stephenson, N.L.; Mutch, L.S.; Johnson, V.G.; Esperanza, A.M.; Parsons, D.J. 2003. Growth rate predicts mortality of *Abies concolor* in both burned and unburned stands. Canadian Journal of Forest Research. 33: 1029–1038.

Wagener, W.W. 1961. Guidelines for estimating the survival of fire damaged trees in California. Misc. Pap. 60. Berkeley, CA: U.S. Department of Agriculture, Forest Service, Pacific Southwest Forest and Range Experiment Station. 11 p.

Wallis, G.W.; Godfrey, J.N.; Richmond, H.A. 1974. Losses in fire-killed timber. Victoria, BC: Pacific Forest Research Center. 11 p.

Wang, B.J.; Dai, C. 2008. Impact of mountain pine beetle-attacked lodgepole pine logs on veneer processing. Wood and Fiber Science. 40(3): 397–411.

Wang, B.J.; Dai, C.; Wharton, S. 2008. Impact of mountain pine beetle-attacked lodgepole pine logs on plywood manufacturing. Wood and Fiber Science. 40(3): 412–426.

Werner, R.A.; Elert, E.E.; Holsten, E.H. 1983. Evaluation of beetle-killed white spruce for pulp and paper. Canadian Journal of Forest Research. 13(2): 246–250.

Western Wood Products Association [WWPA]. 2007. Western price summary December 2007. Report 12. Portland, OR. 9 p.

Wilcox, W.W. 1978. Review of literature on the effects of early stages of decay on wood strength. Wood and Fiber. 9(4): 252–257.

Willits, S.; Sampson, G. 1988. Effects of a forest fire on lumber recovery from white spruce in interior Alaska. Forest Products Journal. 38(11/12): 80–84.

Willits, S.; Woodfin, R.O., Jr.; Snellgrove, T.A. 1990. Lumber recovery from dead ponderosa pine in the Colorado Front Range. Res. Pap. PNW-RP-428. Portland, OR: U.S. Department of Agriculture, Forest Service, Pacific Northwest Research Station. 14 p.

Wright, E.; Coulter, W.K.; Gruenfeld, J.J. 1956. Deterioration of beetle-killed Pacific silver fir. Journal of Forestry. 54(5): 322–325.

Wright, E.; Wright, K.H. 1954. Deterioration of beetle-killed Douglas-fir in Oregon and Washington. Res. Pap. 10. Portland, OR: U.S. Department of Agriculture, Forest Service, Pacific Northwest Forest and Range Experiment Station. 12 p.

Wright, K.H.; Harvey, G.M. 1967. The deterioration of beetle-killed Douglas-fir in western Oregon and Washington. Res. Pap. PNW-50. Portland, OR: U.S. Department of Agriculture, Forest Service, Pacific Northwest Forest and Range Experiment Station. 20 p.

Yadama, V.; Lowell, E.C.; Peterson, N.; Nicholls, D.L. 2009. Wood-plastic composites manufacture using beetle-killed spruce from Alaska's Kenai peninsula. Polymer Science and Engineering. 49(1): 129–136.

Zhong, H.; Schowalter, T.D. 1989. Conifer bole utilization by wood-boring beetles in western Oregon. Canadian Journal of Forestry Research. 19: 943–947.

Appendix 1: Common and Scientific Names

Common name	Scientific name
Trees:	
Douglas-fir	*Pseudotsuga menziesii* (Mirb.) Franco
Engelmann spruce	*Picea engelmanii* Parry ex Engelm.
Grand fir	*Abies grandis* (Douglas ex D. Don) Lindl.
Jeffrey pine	*Pinus jeffreyi* Grev. and Balf.
Lodgepole pine	*Pinus contorta* Dougl. ex Loud.
Lutz spruce	*Picea lutzii* Little
Pacific silver fir	*Abies amabilis* Dougl. ex Forbes
Ponderosa pine	*Pinus ponderosa* Dougl. ex Laws.
Sitka spruce	*Picea sitchensis* (Bong.) Carr.
Subalpine fir	*Abies lasiocarpa* (Hook.) Nutt.
Sugar pine	*Pinus lambertiana* Dougl.
True fir	*Abies* spp.
Western hemlock	*Tsuga heterophylla* (Raf.) Sarg.
Western larch	*Larix occidentalis* Nutt.
Western redcedar	*Thuja plicata* Donn ex D. Don
Western white pine	*Pinus monticola* Dougl. ex D. Don
White fir	*Abies concolor* (Gord. & Glend.) Lindl. ex Hildebr.
White spruce	*Picea glauca* (Moench) Voss
Fungi:	
Blue stain fungi	Genus *Ophiostoma* Syd. & P. Syd. (formerly *Ceratocystis*) (Farr et al. 1989)
	Ophiostoma pseudotsugae (Rumb.) von Arx
	Ophiostoma montium (Rumb.) von Arx
	Ophiostoma clavigerum (Robins.-Jeff., and Davids.) Harrington
Quinine fungus	*Fomitopsis officinalis* (Vill.:Fr.) Bond. & Sing.
Artist's conk	*Ganoderma applanatum* (Pers.) Pat.
No common name	*Gloeophyllum sepiarium* (Wulf.:Fr.) Karst.
No common name	*Trichosporium symbioticum* Wright
No common name—stain fungi	*Ambrosiella* spp.
No common name—stain fungi	*Raffaelae* spp.
Pouch fungus	*Cryptoporus volvatus* (Pk.) Shear.
Purple fungus	*Trichaptum abietinum* (Dicks.:Fr.).
Red belt fungus	*Fomitopsis pinicola* (Sw.:Fr.) Karst.
Red rot fungus	*Dichomitus squalens* (Karst.) Reid
White pine blister rust	*Cronartium ribicola*

Common name	Scientific name
Insects:	
Ambrosia beetle	*Gnathotrichus*
	Monarthrum
	Trypodendron
	Xyleborus
Carpenter ant	*Camponotus* spp.
Douglas-fir bark beetle	*Dendroctonus pseudotsugae* Hopk.
Douglas-fir engraver	*Scolytus unispinosus* LeConte
Douglas-fir tussock moth	*Orgyia pseudotsugata* McDunnough
Fir engraver	*Scolytus ventralis* LeConte
Flatheaded fir borer	*Phaenops drummondi* Kirby
Flatheaded pine borer	*Phaenops gentilis* LeConte
Golden bupestrid	*Buprestis aurulenta* L.
Horntails or woodwasps	Family Siricidae
Jeffrey pine beetle	*Dendroctonus jeffreyi* Hopkins
Mountain pine beetle	*Dendroctonus ponderosae* Hopkins
Pine engraver	*Ips pini* Say
Ponderous borer	*Ergates spiculatus* LeConte
Red turpentine beetle	*Dendroctonus valens* LeConte
Roundheaded borer spp.[a]	*Arhopalus productus* Lec.
	Asemum striatum L.
	Ergates spiculatus LeConte
	Leptura obliterata Hald.
Spruce beetle	*Dendroctonus rufipennis* Kirby
Spruce engraver	*Ips* spp.
Striped ambrosia beetle	*Trypodendron lineatum* Olivier
Western pine beetle	*Dendroctonus brevicomis* LeConte
Western spruce budworm	*Choristoneura occidentalis* Freeman

[a] No common names for individual roundheaded borer species.

Appendix 2: Selected References for Wood Volume/Value Loss by Species

Douglas-fir

Beal, J.A.; Kimmey, J.W.; Rapraeger, E.F. 1935. Deterioration of fire-killed Douglas-fir. The Timberman. 37(2): 12–17.

Bevins, C.D. 1980. Estimating survival and salvage potential of fire-scarred Douglas-fir. Res. Pap. INT-287. Ogden, UT: U.S. Department of Agriculture, Forest Service, Intermountain Forest and Range Experiment Station. 8 p.

Furniss, M.M. 1965. Susceptibility of fire-injured Douglas-fir to bark beetle attack in southern Idaho. Journal of Forestry. 63(1): 8–11.

Kimmey, J.W. 1955. Rate of deterioration of fire-killed timber in California. Circular 962. Washington, DC: U.S. Department of Agriculture. 22 p.

Kimmey, J.W.; Furniss, R.L. 1943. Deterioration of fire-killed Douglas-fir. Tech. Bull. 851. Washington, DC: U.S. Department of Agriculture. 61 p.

Knapp, J.B. 1912. Fire-killed Douglas-fir: a study of its rate of deterioration, usability and strength. Bull. 112. Washington, DC: U.S. Department of Agriculture, Forest Service. 18 p.

Lowell, E.C.; Cahill, J.M. 1996. Deterioration of fire-killed timber in southern Oregon and northern California. Western Journal of Applied Forestry. 11(4): 125–131.

Parry, D.L.; Filip, G.M.; Willits, S.A.; Parks, C.G. 1996. Lumber recovery and deterioration of beetle-killed Douglas-fir and grand fir in the Blue Mountains of eastern Oregon. Gen. Tech. Rep. PNW-GTR-376. Portland, OR: U.S. Department of Agriculture, Forest Service, Pacific Northwest Research Station. 24 p.

Wright, E.; Wright, K.H. 1954. Deterioration of beetle-killed Douglas-fir in Oregon and Washington. Res. Pap. 10. Portland, OR: U.S. Department of Agriculture, Forest Service, Pacific Northwest Forest and Range Experiment Station. 12 p.

Wright, K.H.; Harvey, G.M. 1967. The deterioration of beetle-killed Douglas-fir in western Oregon and Washington. Res. Pap. PNW-50. Portland, OR: U.S. Department of Agriculture, Forest Service, Pacific Northwest Forest and Range Experiment Station. 20 p.

Pine Species

Lodgepole pine—

Dobie, J.; Wright, D.M. 1978. Lumber values from beetle-killed lodgepole pine. Forest Products Journal. 28(6): 44–47.

Fahey, T.D. 1980. Evaluating dead lodgepole pine for products. Forest Products Journal. 30(12): 34–39.

Fahey, T.D.; Snellgrove, T.A.; Plank, M.E. 1986. Changes in product recovery between live and dead lodgepole pine: a compendium. Res. Pap. PNW-353. Portland, OR: U.S. Department of Agriculture, Forest Service, Pacific Northwest Research Station. 25 p.

Forintek Canada Corp. 2006. Rehydrated beetle-killed wood has potential as oriented strandboard feedstock. Specialty Wood Journal. 9(2): 6, 8.

Geiszler, D.R.; Gara, R.I.; Driver, C.H.; Gallucci, V.F.; Martin, R.E. 1980. Fire, fungi and beetle influences on a lodgepole pine ecosystem of south central Oregon. Oecologia. 46: 239–243.

Harvey, R.D., Jr. 1979. Rate of increase of blue stained volume in mountain pine beetle killed lodgepole pine in northeastern Oregon. Canadian Journal of Forest Research. 9(3): 323–326.

Harvey, R.D., Jr. 1986. Deterioration of mountain pine beetle-killed lodgepole pine in northeast Oregon. R6-86-13. Portland, OR: U.S. Department of Agriculture, Forest Service, Pacific Northwest Region.

Ince, P.J.; Henley, J.W.; Grantham, J.B.; Hunt, D.L. 1984. Costs of harvesting beetle-killed lodgepole pine in eastern Oregon. Gen. Tech. Rep. PNW-165. Portland, OR: U.S. Department of Agriculture, Forest Service, Pacific Northwest Research Station. 26 p.

Lemaster, R.L.; Troxell, H.E.; Sampson, G.R. 1983. Wood utilization potential of beetle-killed lodgepole pine for solid wood products. Forest Products Journal. 33(9): 64–68.

Lewis, K.J.; Hartley, I. 2005. Rate of deterioration, degrade and fall of trees killed by mountain pine beetle: a synthesis of the literature and experiential knowledge. Mountain Pine Beetle Initiative Working Paper 2005-14. Victoria, BC: Canadian Forest Service. 27 p.

Littke, W.R.; Gara, R.I. 1986. Decay of fire damaged lodgepole pine in south-central Oregon. Forest Ecology and Management. 17: 279–287.

Maloney, T.M.; Talbott, J.W.; Strickler, M.D.; Lentz, M.T. 1978. Composition board from standing dead white pine and dead lodgepole pine. In: Symposium: The dead softwood timber resource. Pullman, WA: Engineering Extension Service Washington State University: 19–51.

Mitchell, R.G.; Preistler, H.K. 1998. Fall rate of lodgepole pine killed by mountain pine beetle in central Oregon. Western Journal Applied Forestry. 13(1): 23–26.

Nordin, V.J. 1958. Basal fire scars and the occurrence of decay in lodgepole pine. Forestry Chronicles. 34: 257–265.

Plank, M.E. 1979. Lumber recovery from live and dead lodgepole pine in southwestern Wyoming. Res. Note PNW-344. Portland, OR: U.S. Department of Agriculture, Forest Service, Pacific Northwest Forest and Range Experiment Station. 15 p.

Plank, M.E. 1984. Lumber recovery from insect-killed lodgepole pine in the northern Rocky Mountains. Res. Pap. PNW-320. Portland, OR: U.S. Department of Agriculture, Forest Service, Pacific Northwest Forest and Range Experiment Station. 12 p.

Snellgrove, T.A.; Ernst, S. 1983. Veneer recovery from live and dead lodgepole pine. Forest Products Journal. 33(6): 21–26.

Tegethoff, A.C.; Hinds, T.E.; Eslyn, W.E. 1977. Beetle-killed lodgepole pines are suitable for power poles. Forest Products Journal. 27(9): 21–23.

White pine—

Bradner, M.; Anderson, I.V. 1930. Fire-damaged logs—the loss? An analysis of grade depreciation and volume losses of fire-killed Idaho white pine. The Timberman. 1930 (May): 38–43.

Maloney, T.M.; Talbott, J.W.; Strickler, M.D.; Lentz, M.T. 1978. Composition board from standing dead white pine and dead lodgepole pine. In: Symposium: The dead softwood timber resource. Pullman, WA: Engineering Extension Service Washington State University: 19–51.

Snellgrove, T.A.; Cahill, J.M. 1980. Dead western white pine: characteristics, product recovery, and problems associated with utilization. Res. Pap. PNW-270. Portland, OR: U.S. Department of Agriculture, Forest Service, Pacific Northwest Forest and Range Experiment Station. 63 p.

Snellgrove, T.A.; Fahey, T.D. 1977. Market values and problems associated with utilization of dead timber. Forest Products Journal. 27(10): 74–79.

Ponderosa pine—

Connaughton, C.A. 1936. Fire damage in the ponderosa pine type in Idaho. Journal of Forestry. 34(1): 46–51.

Dieterich, J.H. 1979. Recovery potential of fire-damaged southwestern ponderosa pine. Res. Note RN-379. Fort Collins, CO: U.S. Department of Agriculture, Forest Service, Rocky Mountain Forest and Range Experiment Station. 8 p.

Fahey, T.D. 1980. Beetle-killed pine can be salvaged, but for how long? Forest Industries. 107(5): 60–61.

Kimmey, J.W. 1955. Rate of deterioration of fire-killed timber in California. Circular 962. Washington, DC: U.S. Department of Agriculture. 22 p.

Lowell, E.C.; Cahill, J.M. 1996. Deterioration of fire-killed timber in southern Oregon and northern California. Western Journal of Applied Forestry. 11(4): 125–131.

Lowell, E.C.; Parry, D.L. 2007. Value loss in ponderosa pine logs from beetle activity following fire in southern Oregon. Forest Products Journal. 57(7/8): 68–72.

Lynch, D.W. 1959. Effects of a wildfire on mortality and growth of young ponderosa pine trees. Res. Note 66. Ogden, UT: U.S. Department of Agriculture. Forest Service, Intermountain Forest and Range Experiment Station. 8 p.

Miller, J.M.; Patterson, J.E. 1927. Preliminary studies on the relation of fire injury to bark beetle attack in western yellow pine. Journal of Agricultural Research. 34: 597–613.

Willits, S.; Woodfin, R.O., Jr.; Snellgrove, T.A. 1990. Lumber recovery from dead ponderosa pine in the Colorado Front Range. Res. Pap. PNW-RP-428. Portland, OR: U.S. Department of Agriculture, Forest Service, Pacific Northwest Research Station. 14 p.

Other pine species—

Basham, J.T. 1957. The deterioration by fungi of jack, red, and white pine killed by fire in Ontario. Canadian Journal of Botany. 35: 155–172.

Craighead, F.C.; St. George, R.A. 1928. Some effects of fire and insect attack on shortleaf pine. Forest Worker. 4: 11–12.

Kimmey, J.W. 1955. Rate of deterioration of fire-killed timber in California. Circular 962. Washington, DC: U.S. Department of Agriculture. 22 p. (sugar and Jeffrey pines)

Leach, J.G.; Orr, L.W.; Christenson, C. 1934. The interrelationships of bark beetle and blue-staining fungi in felled Norway pine timber. Journal of Agricultural Research. 49(4): 315–341.

Lowell, E.C.; Cahill, J.M. 1996. Deterioration of fire-killed timber in southern Oregon and northern California. Western Journal of Applied Forestry. 11(4): 125–131. (sugar pine)

Spruce Species

Engelmann spruce—

Cahill, J.M. 1980. Preliminary lumber recovery for dead and live Engelmann spruce. Res. Note PNW-365. Portland, OR: U.S. Department of Agriculture, Forest Service, Pacific Northwest Forest and Range Experiment Station. 11 p.

White/Lutz spruce—

Lowell, E.C. 2001. Veneer recovery from beetle-killed spruce trees, Kenai Peninsula, Alaska. Western Journal of Applied Forestry. 16(2): 65–70.

Lowell, E.C.; Willits, S.A. 1998. Lumber recovery from beetle-killed spruce trees on the Kenai Peninsula, Alaska. Western Journal of Applied Forestry. 13(2): 54–59.

Richmond, H.A.; Lejeune, R.R. 1945. The deterioration of fire-killed white spruce by wood boring insects in northern Saskatchewan. Forestry Chronicles. 21: 168–192.

Scott, G.M.; Bormett, D.W.; Sutherland, N.R.; Abubakr, S.; Lowell, E. 1996. Pulpability of beetle-killed spruce. Res. Pap. FPL-RP-557. Madison, WI: U.S. Department of Agriculture, Forest Service, Forest Products Laboratory. 8 p.

Werner, R.A.; Elert, E.E.; Holsten, E. 1983. Evaluation of beetle-killed white spruce for pulp and paper. Canadian Journal of Forest Research. 13(2): 246–250.

Willits, S.; Sampson, G. 1988. Effects of a forest fire on lumber recovery from white spruce in interior Alaska. Forest Products Journal. 38(11/12): 80–84.

True Fir Species

Dobie, J.; Wright, D.M. 1978. Lumber yields and values from dead, standing alpine fir. Forest Products Journal. 28(5): 27–30.

Kimmey, J.W. 1955. Rate of deterioration of fire-killed timber in California. Circular 962. Washington, DC: U.S. Department of Agriculture. 22 p.

Lowell, E.C.; Cahill, J.M. 1996. Deterioration of fire-killed timber in southern Oregon and northern California. Western Journal of Applied Forestry. 11(4): 125–131.

Parry, D.L.; Filip, G.M.; Willits, S.A.; Parks, C.G. 1996. Lumber recovery and deterioration of beetle-killed Douglas-fir and grand fir in the Blue Mountains of eastern Oregon. Gen. Tech. Rep. PNW-GTR-376. Portland, OR: U.S. Department of Agriculture, Forest Service, Pacific Northwest Research Station. 24 p.

Snellgrove, T.A.; Fahey, T.D. 1977. Market values and problems associated with utilization of dead timber. Forest Products Journal. 27(10): 74–79.

Wright, E.; Coulter, W.K.; Gruenfeld, J.J. 1956. Deterioration of beetle-killed Pacific silver fir. Journal of Forestry. 54(5): 322–325.

Appendix 3: Checklist for Field Evaluations of the Wood Quality of Dead and Dying Conifers

Field Worksheet

A worksheet is provided to help managers assess postdisturbance conditions and to develop implications for management. It relies on descriptive stand/site information and on the manager's visual evaluation (and some simple sampling) of eight types of damage. It requires the manager to evaluate average (either for individual trees or across stands) postdisturbance changes relative to a set of reference conditions. These reference conditions are illustrated in figure 18. The manager is asked to consider the conditions found in the bottom, middle, and top third of the tree bole affected by each of the eight damage agents.

Ranking each condition relative to the reference condition (shown in each photo) as less, the same as, or more than, leads to a rating system that aids in developing management suggestions. In using the worksheet, the manager rates the condition of each damage agent relative to the reference conditions. A value of 1 is for tree/stand condition more damaged than shown in the reference photo. A value of 2 is for tree/stand condition the same as reference condition. A value of 3 is for tree/stand less damaged than the reference condition or the damage is not present. This evaluation is repeated for the three sections of each tree bole, as some damage agents are more specific to either the tops or bases of trees (see tables 2 through 6).

The evaluation itself provides structure to describing postdisturbance conditions, and also provides the basis for developing suggestions for managing postdisturbance stands, especially when considering the possibilities of active forest management practices. The first step is summing up the scores from the ratings (a maximum of 72 is possible). For stands less damaged than the reference conditions (total ratings of 56 or more) and where timber sales are possible, it is possible to use active forest management implemented with sawtimber harvest to restore function. Where timber sales are not possible, these stands will follow successional pathways, albeit more slowly. For those stands damaged much like shown in the reference conditions (total ratings of 40 to 55) recovery of predisturbance conditions is less assured. In those stands where timber sales are possible there may be enough volume in butt logs to enable timber sales for both sawtimber and nonsawtimber[5] products. Such sales can enable hazardous fuel reduction treatments as well as efforts to develop other environmental services such as wildlife habitat. Where timber sales are not possible, thought should be given to minimalistic approaches

---

[5] Nonsawtimber products are chips, house logs, posts, poles, and firewood.

Figure 18—These photos are to be used in conjunction with the field worksheet for assessing postdisturbance changes to evaluate tree condition for utilization opportunities. Photos represent the reference condition that is assigned a value of 2 on the rating scale in appendix 3 for the following visual characteristics: (A) crown condition (B) bark loss (C) weather check (D) breakage (E) beetle activity (F) stain (G) conks and (H) char.

to hazardous fuel treatments and protection of environmental services. For those stands more severely damaged than the reference conditions (total ratings of 39 or less), recovery will be difficult. Even where timber sales are possible, the small volumes of sawtimber and large volumes of nonsawtimber limit the opportunities to use timber sales to facilitate hazardous fuel treatments or management for other environmental services.

Worksheet for Assessing Postdisturbance Changes

Site		Primary species	
Elevation		Age	
Aspect		Size	
If fire, how long ago		% Sapwood	

Evidence of disturbance agents			
Extent of damage	Bottom third of tree	Middle third of tree	Top third of tree
(a) Crown condition			
(b) Bark loss			
(c) Weather checking			
(d) Breakage, large limb loss			
(e) Beetle activity			
(f) Stain in sapwood			
(g) Fungus/conks			
(h) Char			

Rating system

1—If the tree/stand condition is more damaged than shown in the reference photo.

2—If the tree/stand condition is the same as reference condition.

3—If the tree/stand is less damaged than the reference condition or if the damage is not present.

Management implications		
Total ratings	Timber sales possible	Timber sales not possible
56–72	Use active forest management implemented with sawtimber harvest to restore function.	Successional patterns will be slowed by increased mortality in these stands.
40–55	There may be enough volume in butt logs to enable timber sales for both sawtimber and nonsawtimber products.	It might be possible to use minimalistic approaches for hazardous fuel treatments and enhancement of environmental services.
24–39	The small volumes of sawtimber and large volumes of nonsawtimber limit the opportunities to use timber sales to facilitate hazardous fuel or environmental services management.	Recovery is a function of successional patterns. Stands may require expensive hazardous fuel treatments.